EVERYDAY FAVORITES FROM THE STREET TO THE KITCHEN

REAL
VIETNAMESE
COOKING

YUMIKO ADACHI, SHINOBU ITO
and MASUMI SUZUKI

TUTTLE Publishing

Tokyo | Rutland, Vermont | Singapore

Contents

Rice Paper Dishes

Rice Noodles & More

Bánh Mì Sandwiches

Rice Flour Dishes

Casual Restaurant Dining

Pub Food & Bar Snacks

Salads & Vegetables

Vietnamese Hot Pots

Rice Dishes

Snacks, Desserts & Drinks

The Origins of Vietnamese Cuisine

by Shinobu Ito

Northern Origins

From a historical standpoint, it's northern Vietnamese cuisine that can be considered "traditional." There are 54 different ethnic groups in Vietnam; the largest, the Kinhs or Viets, originally occupied the North. Until the 17th century, the central part of the country was occuped by the Cham and the South by the Khmer. The Cham and Khmer still live in Vietnam as ethnic minorities, and collectively these influences intersect to create contemporary Vietnamese cuisine.

The Cham and the Khmer

Today, fish sauce (nước mắm) is an essential element in Vietnamese cuisine. It was originally introduced by the Cham, a seafaring people from present-day Malaysia and Indonesia. The climate of central Vietnam is ideally suited to growing chili peppers. This is why many central Vietnamese dishes are quite spicy.

The Khmer in the South founded the current country of Cambodia. They were strongly influenced by Indian culture, so southern Vietnamese cuisine is characterized by its use of lots of spices. There are Vietnamese dishes referred to as "curry," but they're only eaten in the South. There are quite a lot of dishes that are eaten in southern and central Vietnam that aren't seen in the North, further evidence of the influence of Cham and Khmer culture on the diversity of Vietnamese cuisine.

The Influence of Chinese Immigrants

Aside from the influence of the centuries-long Chinese occupation, the influx of immigrants from China has been equally profound. There were two major waves of immigration from China to Vietnam: one in the mid-17th century, and another in the mid-19th to early 20th centuries. Many immigrants became citizens during those times. Around the 16th century, Chinatowns were established in the central Vietnamese cities of Hội An and Da Nang, thriving as immigrant communities up until the French colonial period. Chinese also settled in the southern Mekong delta in the 19th century. These immigrants and their descendents have left a lasting mark on the regional cuisines of Vietnam.

Climate and Produce Vary by Region

Northern Vietnam has a subtropical climate and four distinct seasons. Sometimes the temperatures in the winter go below 50°F (10°C). The southern region has a tropical monsoon climate and is hot year-round, with just two seasons: rainy and dry. The central region has both rainy and dry seasons; it's cold in the rainy season, and blisteringly hot in the dry season.

Geographically the North is very mountainous, the central region is along the coastline, while the South has many swamps. While the North and South have large rivers to supply freshwater fish, saltwater fish are popular in the coastal central region. In the North, root vegetables and potatoes are common, while in the South vegetables such as eggplants, cucumbers and squash are cultivated. Climate and geographical difference mean that the ingredients and flavors of each region differ, making for a varied and rich food culture.

What Do the Vietnamese Eat?

by Shinobu Ito

Here are some typical examples of what the Vietnamese eat in a day.

Breakfast

Eating out is very popular in Vietnam. Breakfast is one meal that's usually eaten outside the home. A light meal, it rarely features plain rice. The sole exception is cơm tấm, a snack-like dish made with broken rice grains, eaten with marinated pork or other highly flavored additions. Besides that, phở and other noodle dishes, flour-based staples such as steamed meat buns, rice-flour-based items such as rice porridge and sticky sweet rice, sandwiches and bread are eaten for breakfast.

Lunch

For the Vietnamese, a meal consists of plain white rice and the dishes that go with it. For lunch, white rice, a main side dish consisting of meat or fish, a soup packed with vegetables, plus other side dishes made with eggs, tofu, seafood and vegetables are eaten. Although noodle dishes such as Bún Chả Giò (page 47) and Mì Quảng Gà (page 56) are eaten sometimes for lunch, this meal is usually centered on white rice. The main side dishes are well-flavored, to go with the plain white rice. When the soup is made at home, it usually has a ton of vegetables in it. Pickles, which also go well with rice, are often included too. If eating lunch out, people typically go to a casual restaurant (pages 92–93; the equivalent of a diner) and order a main side dish, soup and other sides a la carte. In the Casual Restaurant Dining section (pages 92–107), we show you how to make some typical dishes served at these traditional eateries.

Daytime Snacks

In Vietnam, sweet and savory snacks are eaten in between the morning, midday and evening meals. These are called ăn nhẹ (light meal), điểm tâm (dim sum) and ăn vặt (snack). Sweet snacks include chè, a Vietnamese-style sweet beverage, dessert soup or pudding. Fresh fruit is eaten as a snack too.

Typical snack foods include noodle dishes, wheat- and rice-flour items, porridge, sticky rice, sandwiches and the breads eaten for breakfast. All of these snack foods are eaten at speciality restaurants, food stalls or are purchased from street vendors who sell from their bicycles or from containers carried on their shoulders on poles.

Dinner or Evening Meal

Dinners eaten at home are similar to lunch, centered on plain white rice with side dishes plus soup that goes with the rice. Quán cơm bình dân are mainly for lunch; even though some are also open for dinner, most close early. There are pubs that serve light meals with bia hơi or draught beer (page 109), as well as hot-pot eateries, full-service restaurants, street stalls selling grilled chicken skewers and various eateries that specialize in certain foods.

Feasts

When the whole family gets together on the weekends or when everyone has free time, or when there are honored guests, special long-cooked meals are prepared. On those occasions, instead of the plain white rice eaten at everyday meals, the prepared dishes are often eaten with bún (rice noodles) or wrapped in rice paper. Food like this is called món ăn ngày Chủ Nhật, or "Sunday cooking." Everyday white rice is not served at special occasions like weddings and banquets either. If rice is on the menu, something requiring extra effort, such as fried rice, is served. Food at these large gatherings used to be served on big platters placed all at once on the table, but after the French colonial period, course-style meal service was incorporated.

All About Vietnamese Seasonings

Shinobu Ito

A variety of seasonings are key to Vietnamese cuisine. Some specialized ingredients may be harder to find locally and only available online, but here I'd like to introduce you to the ones most commonly used in everyday Vietnamese cooking.

Fish Sauce Nước mắm

A fermented fish sauce made from anchovies mixed with salt, packed into barrels or large pots and allowed to ferment for six months to a year (or sometimes longer). The clear liquid produced by lactic acid fermentation is nước mắm. The first liquid skimmed off is called first-press nước mắm (nước mắm cốt, nước mắm nhĩ). Water is added to fish left over after the first-press nước mắm has been taken out to make second-press and later nước mắm. All nước mắm has something called an N number, which indicates the level of nitrogen. The higher the number, the more umami the nước mắm is judged to have, and the better the quality.

ese cooking after nước mắm. It tastes quite different from the basic soy sauce brands sold in North American supermarkets, but if you can't get Vietnamese soy sauce, use Thai or Vietnamese seasoning sauce instead.

Vietnamese Soy Sauce Xì dầu Nước tương

Soy sauce was introduced to Vietnam by Chinese immigrants from Guangdong. Soy beans are fermented, and umami flavorings and sweeteners are added. Soy sauce is the second-most-used seasoning in Vietnam-

Fermented Soy Bean Paste Tương

There are several villages in northern and central Vietnam that are famous for their versions of miso, or fermented soy bean paste. Salt water is added during the process, for a more liquid consistency. It's used as a dipping sauce, as well as a flavoring ingredient in soups. In the South, a sweet, black sauce called tương đen, similar to hoisin sauce, was introduced by Chinese immigrants, and is used as a dipping sauce for fresh spring rolls or added to phở.

Fermented Seafood Pastes Mắm

Mắm is the word for all types of fermented seafood pastes. They include mắm tôm, a fermented shrimp paste used in the North; mắm ruốc, made with a tiny krill-like shrimp called acetes in central Vietnam; and mắm cá thu, made in the South with freshwater fish.

Chili Sauces Tường ớt & Tường ớt chua ngọt

There are hot and spicy chili sauces and sweet chili sauces. The hot ones (tương ớt) are made by simmering red chili peppers, sugar, vinegar, garlic and tomatoes and turning the result into a paste. (Some types don't include tomatoes.) It's added to phở before eating, used as a dipping sauce for squid or deep-fried foods and added to bánh mì. Sweet chili sauce (tương ớt chua ngọt) is made by adding water and sugar to chopped red chili peppers, garlic, vinegar and salt, and simmered until reduced or thickened with starch. It's thinned out and used as a sauce, or used as is as a dip for deep-fried foods.

Sugar Đường

Granulated sugar is most commonly used in Vietnamese cooking, but brown sugar, rock sugar and palm sugar are also used. For the sweet-sour sauces made with nước mắm, granulated sugar is the best; brown sugar is the choice for stewed dishes; and rock sugar is ideal for making chè. Palm sugar is made in the Mekong delta in southern Vietnam, and is used a lot in the dishes from that region.

Vinegar Giấm, Dấm

The popular types of vinegar used in Vietnam are made from rice, sweet rice or banana. Most commercially sold vinegars are blends, so a lot of people make their own. In general, Vietnamese vinegars are mild.

A Street Food Paradise

by Yumiko Adachi

An Infinite Number of Dishes

If you walk around the streets of any town or city in Vietnam, you'll encounter food stalls selling snacks all day long. Besides stationary stalls, there are also vendors who go around on bicycles or on foot, setting up shop temporarily to sell snacks on the street. There are sweet snacks—such as chè, coconut and banana cakes, ice cream and puddings—and a range of savory snacks too: Bột Chiên (page 85), Bánh Tráng Nướng (page 27), Bánh Tráng Trộn (page 29), Gỏi Cuốn or fresh spring rolls (page 31), Bắp Xào (page 155), green papaya salads, fried fish cakes and deep-fried Nem chua, a fermented sausage, plus countless other snacks to enjoy. I've been going to Vietnam several times a year for 20 years, and each time I encounter a snack I've never had before.

Students Are in the Know

If you want to try a variety of snacks, aim for the areas near schools. Every day around the time school lets out, a number of food stalls suddenly pop up near the school gates. There are sweet snacks that use coconut and yogurt, as well as savory snacks assembled and fried to order. Go just before school is done for the day before the kids start lining up, and buy as many snacks as you want.

I always wish that I could enjoy a beer as I nibble on a fried fish cake, but as these stalls cater to kids, alcohol isn't sold.

Vietnamese Coffee and Tea

by Shinobu Ito

Green Tea Is Popular in Vietnam

Tea used to be reserved for the upper classes and only served to guests, but these days it's enjoyed as an everyday beverage. In Vietnam, green tea is the most popular type. Fragrant jasmine and lotus flower teas are also widely popular. Vietnamese tea is brewed in a pot, typically made strong and dark, then sipped slowly from tiny cups. In the hotter regions, iced tea is enjoyed too. In northern cities such as Hanoi, if there's a low plastic chair and a warmer for a tea pot on the side of the street, then you've found a teahouse.

French-Influenced Café Society

In contrast to the North, in southern cities such as Hồ Chí Minh City, simple teahouses don't exist. However there are streetside coffee vendors who will serve you tea after your coffee. That beverage entered Vietnam

in the 17th and 18th centuries, but it only became established after the French occupation, starting in 1857. The first place where coffee culture established itself was in Hồ Chí Minh City, where the French built two cafés exclusively for their own use. In the 1900s, the Vietnamese adopted the habit of drinking coffee too, and the number of cafés increased. Vietnamese coffee is of the dark French-roasted type, dripped slowly through an aluminum filter. Originally there were just two types: hot coffee with sugar and iced coffee. Later on, coffee with condensed milk added was introduced and became the standard. There are cafés serving coffee everywhere in Vietnam. The nation not only adopted the coffee-drinking habit from France, they also inherited its café culture.

Useful Kitchen Tools Sold in Vietnam

Water Spinach Cutter

A tool for finely shredding the stems of water spinach (also called kangkong, rau muong or ong choy). The skewer is inserted into the hollow stem (**photo a**), and then the stem is pulled through (**b-c**). There are several blades arranged in a spiral at the top (**d**); by pulling the stem through them, it's thinly shredded.

Wavy Vegetable Slicer

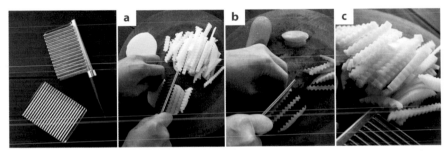

A knife with a wavy blade. There are types with or without handles. The ones without handles are helds like a dough scraper in your hand. These are used to cut carrots and daikon radish (**photos a-b**) for crinckle-cut vegetables. (**c**).

Crinkle-Cutting Knife

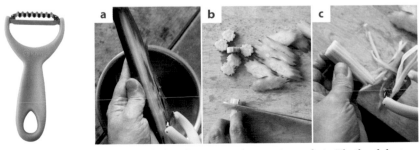

A vegetable peeler with a wavy blade. This particular one is made in Thailand, but you can buy similar ones in Vietnam too. Use this to peel cucumbers and carrots thinly (**photo a**) so that the surface becomes wavy, then slice to make wavy-edged pieces (**b**). Use as a peeler to shred the vegetable (**c**).

Herbs and Aromatics

What's the most distinctive quality of Vietnam's cuisine? That's easy: the herbs and vegetables. Some are hard to find, so substituting locally sourced mint, cilantro, shallots or scallions is fine.

Coriander Leaves/Cilantro
rau mùi in the North; ngò rí in the South A lot of people assume that coriander leaves or cilantro is used in every Vietnamese dish, but that's not necessarily the case; just a lot of them. In Vietnamese homes, it's used in soups and as a garnish on noodle dishes. It's not used that much in rice-paper-wrapped meat, seafood and vegetable dishes.

Asian or Thai Basil rau húng
in the North; húng quế in the South This is the same type of basil used in Thailand. This fragrant, purple-stemmed herb is essential for south-ern-style phở. It's also added to many other noodle dishes and is often stacked high on the dinner table where people can take as much as they like. It's always used in rice-paper-wrapped dishes in the South, in particular.

Mint húng lủi also called bạc
hà in the North It is often used in rice-paper-wrapped dishes, as well as mixed noodle dishes like bún and salads. Although húng lủi is the name of spear-mint, the northern term bạc hà is used over all for different kinds of mint.

Vietnamese Perilla tía tô
The perilla leaves used in Vietnam are rounder than Japanese shiso, have a much stronger fragrance and are bronze-green on the front side and red-purple on the back side. Perilla is used in rice-paper-wrapped dishes, chopped up and added to the stewed eggplant dishes of the North and added to river snail and shellfish dishes.

Thorny Coriander/Cilantro
mùi tàu in the North; ngò gai in the South Also known as Mexican or sawtooth corian-der, a very strongly flavored herb with serrated-edged leaves. It's an essential herb in some southern-style phở, and since it matches well with beef, it's used in mixed beef salad dishes too. It's chopped finely and added to southern củ mài (yam) soups.

Dill thìa là in the North; thì là
in the South Dill was intro-duced to Vietnam during the French colonial period, and became well-established as a crop in the North, where the climate is ideal for growing it. It goes especially well with fish and tomato-based dishes and is used a lot in the North with thin green onions.

Betel Leaf/Lolot Pepper lá lốt
There's no official English name for this common herb used throughout Southeast Asia, but you may see it sold as one of the names listed in the heading. The botanical name is *Piper sarmentosum* or *Piper lolot*. It's a very fragrant herb; the chopped beef and mixed herb dish bò lá lốt is made with it, where the leaves are used to wrap the beef. It's also popular-ly used to wrap various kinds of chopped meat, as well as as a topping for noodles.

Vietnamese Balm kinh giới
The botanical name is *Elsholt-zia ciliata*. Similar to perilla, but with a stronger, distinctive fragrance, it's used a lot in northern noodle dishes. If you can't find it, we recommend substituting perilla, shiso or lemonbalm leaves.

Vietnamese Coriander rau răm
Also called Vietnamese mint,

Asian or Thai Basil

Thorny Coriander

Perilla

Vietnamese Coriander

Vietnamese cilantro, Cambodian mint, hot mint, laksa leaf or praew leaf. The botanical name is *Persicaria odorata*. It has a spicy bite and a strong fragrance. Since it's believed to have detoxifying qualities, it's always served with shelfish or organ dishes and balut (boiled unhatched duck embryos). In the South, it's often used to scent salad-style dishes too.

Fish Mint/Chameleon Plant
giáp cá in the North; diếp cá in the South Because of its rather raw fishy fragrance, it is called fish leaf or fish herb in Vietnam. The botanical name is *Houttuynia cordata*. It's often used in rice-paper- or lettuce-leaf-wrapped dishes. In the South, it's added to bánh xèo and fresh spring rolls too.

Lemongrass sả
Lemongrass has the same substance that gives lemons their fragrance. In Vietnam, the stalk is chopped finely and stir fried until crisp in oil, mixed with other aromatic vegetables and herbs to flavor meats and fish or steamed with fish.

Chili Pepper ớt
First introduced to central Vietnam, it's now used around the country. There are several varieties by region, with different flavors and levels of heat. Both ripe, red chili peppers and immature green ones

are used. Besides being used fresh, dried and powdered chili peppers are used in the central and mountain regions.

Garlic tỏi
The Vietnamese version is small and rather mild.

Scallions or Green Onions
hành lá Thin green onions or scallions are all collectively called hành lá. They're indispensable to Vietnamese cuisine, chopped and added as a finishing garnish to soups, noodles and other dishes. In the North they're chopped roughly and used abundantly in soups and other dishes. Mở hành or onion oil, made by pouring hot oil or fat over chopped green onions, is commonly used.

Red Shallots
hành khôin the North; hành tím in the South Called hom dang in Thai, this is a red-purple cross between shallots and onions. The bulb is often sliced and dried for long keeping. It has a pleasant fragrance, so it's often cooked with garlic to transfer its flavor to the oil, and used in stews and stir-fried dishes. The ready-made fried onions used in this book are ideally the deep-fried version of this flavorful shallot.

Vietnamese Lime chanh
Vietnamese limes are small

and round, the same variety as key limes and Thai manao limes. They have a refreshing fragrance and tartness, and are combined with nước mắm and sugar to make a sweet-sour sauce, or are squeezed over soup noodles. You can easily substitute regular limes or lemons.

Ginger Root gừng
The same as the ginger root you can get anywhere, although it tends to be a bit drier.

Galangal/Thai Ginger riềng
The same as the root called kà in Thai. Similar to ginger, this is indispensable to northern Vietnamese cooking. It has a stronger, distinctive fragrance compared to ginger, and is often used with stewed freshwater fish as well as in marinades for meat.

Kaffir Lime Leaf/Makrut Lime Leaf lá chanh
These leaves have a very refreshing fragrance and are used, as is, finely shredded in chicken and river snail dishes.

Vietnamese Chives củ nén
A member of the chive faily, it forms small bulbs similar to shallots underground. It's indispensable to the cuisine of central Vietnam, especially the city of Hue.

Garlic   Scallions or Green Onions   Red Shallots   Vietnamese Limes

Glossary of Vietnamese Seasonings

Fish Sauce

Vietnamese fish sauce (nước mắm), made by fermenting salted fish. The saltiness and flavor differ from brand to brand, so be sure to taste an unfamiliar one before using it. The southern Vietnamese island of Phú Quốc is especially renowned for producing nước mắm. In this book, we've used the nước mắm from Phú Quốc, pictured here.

Hot Chili Sauce

A hot and spicy sauce made by cooking red chili peppers and garlic into a paste with added seasonings. We recommend using a Vietnamese brand, which you can get from Asian or Vietnamese grocery stores. It can be used on its own as a dipping sauce, added to finished dishes or served with noodle soups. See page 9.

Fried Onions

Deep-fried red shallots (page 13). Both Vietnamese and Thai varieties can be found in Asian grocery stores. They're sprinkled over noodles and salads and taste quite different from the version made with regular onions (that are used in Chinese cooking for example), so try and locate a Southeast Asian variety.

Fresh Coriander Leaves or Cilantro

A herb with a distinctive fragrance and an addictive flavor. See page 12.

Thai or Vietnamese Seasoning Sauce

This soy bean sauce (soy sauce) is used nearly as much as nước mắm in Vietnamese cooking. If you can't locate Vietnamese brands, look for Thai ones instead. Sugar and umami flavorings are added to the soy sauce, giving it a sweet finish.

Tamarind Pulp or Paste

This is made from the fruit or pods of the tamarind tree. Besides fresh pods, tamarind is available in several forms, including the one shown here: a block of the pulp including seeds and all. This is sometimes sold as "wet tamarind." It's soaked in water to soften for about 20 minutes, then shredded or pulled apart and/or passed through a sieve to eliminate the seeds and turn it into a smooth paste. The other type is a ready-to-use paste, sold in jars, tubes or pouches. Tamarind has a refreshing tartness. You can also get frozen tamarind pulp. In this book, we use compressed tamarind pulp.

Scallions or Green Onions

The green parts are used as garnish and toppings, and the white part is used as an aromatic vegetable.

Mint Leaves

A staple of the Vietnamese kitchen, especially for North American chefs, where perilla leaves are hard to find. Mint makes the ideal substitute.

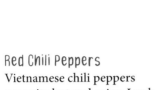

Red Chili Peppers

Vietnamese chili peppers are quite hot and spicy. Look around at your local supermarket and farmers' markets, as well as Asian groceries, to see what types of chili peppers are available. If you can find ones labeled for Vietnamese cooking that's great, but ones meant for Thai cooking are fine as substitutes. You may also be able to find frozen Thai chili peppers.

Kaffir or Makrut Lime Leaves

Use fresh leaves. They're available at Asian grocery stores, especially ones that cater to South or Southeast Asian shoppers. They can be frozen. See page 13.

Thai or Asian Basil

Sometimes called holy basil. If you can't find it, sweet basil can be substituted. See page 12.

Lemongrass

Use fresh stalks. The usable part is about 8 inches (20 cm) from the root end. It can also be frozen. See page 13.

Green Mangoes

Unripe mangoes are used as a vegetable. The fruit is yellow with a subtle sweetness and a strong sour tang. They're harder than ripe mangoes. Green mangoes are available at South or Southeast Asian grocery stores.

Green Papayas

Unripe papayas are used as a vegetable. The fruit is hard and crispy, used in salads and as a garnish. Green papayas are increasingly available at regular supermarkets, as well as Southeast Asian grocery stores.

Red Shallots

A gift of the French, red shallots grow wild throughout Southeast Asia, where they're sliced thin and deep fried for a crunchy condiment.

Basic Recipes Used Throughout This Book

Nước Chấm Dressing or Dipping Sauce

Version A by Yumiko Adachi
3 tablespoons sugar
6 tablespoons hot water
2 tablespoons nước mắm
2 tablespoons lemon juice
½ garlic clove, minced
½ red chili pepper, minced

Version B by Yumiko Adachi
3 tablespoons sugar
6 tablespoons hot water
2 tablespoons nước mắm
1 tablespoon lemon juice

Version C by Masumi Suzuki
3 tablespoons sugar
2 tablespoons cold water
2 tablespoons nước mắm
3 tablespoons lemon juice
½ garlic clove, minced
⅓ red chili pepper, minced

For each variation: Dissolve the sugar in the specified amount of water, then add the rest of the ingredients and mix. Although all dressings and sauces are called "nước chấm," in this book we've used it to specify the sauce that's made with nước mắm, lemon juice and sugar as the base. The amounts here are just guidelines. Lemons vary in acidity, so be sure to taste and adjust the amount every time you make this.

Green Onion Oil

Version A by Yumiko Adachi
3 tablespoons chopped green onions
1 pinch salt
4 tablespoons vegetable oil

Version B by Shinobu Ito
2 to 3 stalks green onions, chopped
1 pinch salt
1 tablespoon vegetable oil

Version C by Masumi Suzuki
4 tablespoons chopped green onions
4 tablespoons canola oil

For each variation: Put the chopped green onion in a heatproof container, and add the salt. Heat the oil in a frying pan, pour into the container with the green onion and mix rapidly.

Northern Vietnamese-Style Pickles

Shinobu Ito

3 cups (300 g) total green papaya and carrots (you can substitute daikon radish for the green papaya)
3 tablespoons sugar
2 tablespoons rice vinegar

1 Slice the green papaya and carrot thinly against the grain of each vegetable.
2 Add the sugar and vinegar to the vegetables, and mix well with your hands. Leave for 30 minutes, and squeeze out the excess moisture before serving.

Marinated Daikon Radish and Carrot
Yumiko Adachi

¼ lb (120 g) peeled daikon radish
½ cup (50 g) peeled carrot
1 pinch salt
2 tablespoons hot water
2 tablespoons sugar
2 tablespoons rice vinegar

1 Cut the daikon radish and carrot into matchsticks using a wavy blade knife. Sprinkle with salt and leave for a few minutes.
2 Dissolve the sugar in the hot water. Add the vinegar and mix.
3 Squeeze out the vegetables tightly to remove excess moisture. Marinate in the sugar-vinegar dressing for about 15 minutes.

Pickled Green Papaya and Carrot
Yumiko Adachi

⅔ cup (120 g) shredded green papaya
½ cup (50 g) shredded carrot
1 pinch salt
1⅓ tablespoons hot water
1⅓ tablespoons sugar
2 tablespoons rice vinegar

1 Combine the green papaya and carrot in a bowl, sprinkle with salt and leave for a few minutes.
2 Dissolve the sugar in the hot water. Add the vinegar and mix.
3 Squeeze out the vegetables tightly to remove excess moisture. Marinate in the sugar-vinegar dressing for about 15 minutes.

Southern Vietnamese-Style Pickles
Shinobu Ito

3 cups (300 g) total daikon radish and carrots
1 teaspoon salt
2 tablespoons hot water
2 tablespoons sugar
2 tablespoons rice vinegar

1 Cut the daikon radish and carrots into matchsticks. (Use a wavy blade knife if you have one: see page 11). Sprinkle the vegetables with the salt, and leave for about 5 minutes.
2 When the vegetables have wilted, rinse them, changing the water 2 to 3 times. Squeeze the vegetables tightly to remove excess moisture.
3 In a separate bowl, dissolve the sugar in the hot water, add the vinegar and mix. Combine the vinegar-sugar dressing with the vegetables in a bowl, and put a plate on top with a can or similar object as a weight. Leave to marinate for about 30 minutes.

Daikon Radish and Carrot Marinated in Nước Chấm
Masumi Suzuki

¼ lb (100 g) peeled daikon radish
½ cup (50 g) peeled carrot
1 scant teaspoon salt
3 tablespoons Nước Chấm, Version C (page 16)

1 Cut the daikon radish and carrot into matchsticks using a wavy blade knife. Sprinkle with salt and leave for a few minutes.
2 Rinse the vegetables in water, and squeeze tightly to remove excess moisture. Combine with the nước chấm and marinate for 2 to 3 hours.

RICE PAPER DISHES

Rice paper isn't just for spring rolls!

Types of Vietnamese Rice Paper

While circular rice papers are the most common, if you find the square kind, pick them up and start thinking inside the box.

Round Rice Papers

Round rice paper is made by rolling rice dough very thinly, steaming it and then drying it on bamboo sieves. There are two sizes, one that's about 8 inches (20 cm) in diameter, and one that's about 6 inches (15 cm). Most round rice paper is made of tapioca flour as well as rice flour, so it needs to be moistened or immersed in water before using.

Square Rice Papers

This is very thin rice paper, originally made in northern Vietnam. Since it's so thin it doesn't need to be moistened before using, and can be used as is to wrap around vegetables, meat and seafood since it's softened by the ingredients inside. Use round rice paper if you can't find square.

Shinobu Ito According to legend, rice paper was first made during the Tây Sơn dynasty, during the reign of Emperor Quang Trung (Nguyễn Huệ), to feed a hungry army on the go. It's best known as a wrapper for fresh spring rolls (gỏi cuốn), a light snack that's eaten in a part of southern Vietnam only. The most popular way to use rice paper is to wrap meat, fish, vegetables and herbs in it at the table. In recent years, new ways to enjoy rice paper, such as for Bánh Tráng Nướng (page 27) and Bánh Tráng Trộn (page 29), have also appeared.

Masumi Suzuki Rice paper is best known outside Vietnam as a wrapper for fresh or deep-fried spring rolls, while its other uses aren't widely known. When diners at my restaurant use it to wrap meat, fish and vegetables for the first time, they're overjoyed, saying, "I didn't know you could use rice paper like this!"

Yumiko Adachi The first time I had rice paper in Vietnam, I was really surprised at how much thinner it was than the type I'd had in Japan. In Vietnam, it's often used without dipping it in water first. Sometimes it is sandwiched between banana leaves, to allow the moisture from the leaves to soften it before using.

How to Prepare Rice Papers

Less is more when it comes to moistening your rice papers. You'll soon get the hang of it, but be careful not to oversaturate them, or you'll have a soggy circle of goo in your hands.

Reconstituting Rice Paper

Fill a bowl with water and briefly immerse a rice paper in it (**photo a**). Some types of rice paper will become too soft if you do this. If you find this to be the case with the rice paper you have, brush it with water instead (**b**). Place the moistened rice paper briefly on a plate, board or tray covered with a kitchen towel, to allow the moisture in the rice paper to become evenly absorbed. When the rice paper is soft enough not to break when folded or handled, it's ready to use to encase your choice of ingredients.

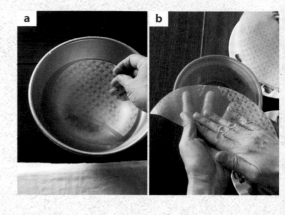

Rice-Paper Gadgets in Vietnam

In Vietnam, there are various gadgets available for reconstituting rice paper. **Photo a** shows round plastic nets for soaking several sheets at once. The rice paper is layered alternately with the plastic net, and the stack is passed through the water all at once and brought to the table. The far-right photo (**b**) shows a container for passing rice paper through water. A sheet of rice paper is placed inside and turned around once to wet it.

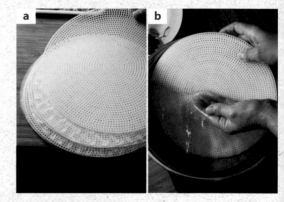

How the Fresh Spring Roll Was Born

by Shinobu Ito

Southern Treats

Fresh spring rolls, or gỏi cuốn (page 31), are so famous outside Vietnam that they're often thought of as the quintessential Vietnamese dish by foreigners. However, in reality they're only eaten in southern Vietnam, in and around Hồ Chí Minh City (formerly Saigon). You do see them occasionally in tourist-oriented restaurants in northern and central Vietnam, but it's not something eaten every day by local people in these regions.

Fresh spring rolls were born during the time of the French occupation, in the Chợ Lớn district of Ho Chí Minh City, once a neighborhood heavily occupied by Chinese immigrants. So they're not a traditional dish, but relatively new to the Vietnamese table, influenced by the tastes of other countries. In order to introduce you to how the fresh spring roll was born, I have to start with the Chinese-style fresh spring rolls, bò bía (page 32).

From China's Popiah to Vietnam's Bò Bía

The base for Vietnam's bò bía is the Chinese popiah, a roll made with a thin, wheat-flour skin (also called a popiah) spread with a fermented soybean paste, filled with raw or cooked vegetables, rolled and deep fried. This type of spring roll was introduced to other parts of Asia by the Chinese immigrants who settled in Taiwan, Singapore, Malaysia and Thailand. In those countries, it's known by variations on the name popiah: such as po pia and po phia. The wrapper or skin is usually made with wheat flour, but in southern Chinese rice-producing provinces, such as Fujian and Guangdong, rice-based wrappers are used.

The Chinese immigrants who settled in the Chợ Lớn district and introduced popiah to Vietnam were mainly from Chaozhou in Guangdong. In the Chaozhou dialect, apparently popiah is pronounced as "bo-bi-a," and from that the Vietnamese named the dish bò bía. Vietnamese people preferred using the rice-paper wrappers they already ate over the fried skins of the original popiah, so the rice-paper-wrapped Vietnamese-style version was born.

Locally Inspired Variations

Inspired by Vietnamese-style popiah or bò bía, local restaurants started serving rolls using fillings familiar to and preferred by the Vietnamese people: boiled shrimp and pork, raw vegetables, herbs and bún (noodles). This version quickly took over, and thus the "fresh spring roll" was born. They're typically served with a miso sauce in Vietnam because the condiment is based on the miso paste put inside the original Chinese popiah, the ancestor of the gỏi cuốn or fresh spring roll.

Deep-Fried Spring Rolls Chả giò

Yumiko Adachi

Southern Vietnamese-style spring rolls like these are quite small. They're eaten wrapped with lots of fresh herbs in lettuce leaves.

Makes 20 rolls

1 tablespoon dried wood ear mushrooms
½ oz (15 g) dried mung bean cellophane
    or glass noodles
20 small round rice paper wrappers,
    passed through water to soften
Oil, for deep frying
Nước Chấm, Version A (page 16), to taste
Lettuce leaves and herbs (mint, coriander
    leaves/cilantro), to taste

Filling
½ lb (225 g) ground pork
⅛ cup (55 g) flaked crabmeat
2 garlic cloves, minced
½ egg
½ teaspoon sugar
¼ teaspoon salt
2 teaspoons freshly ground black pepper

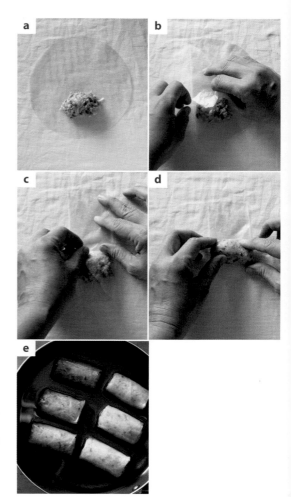

1 Soak the wood ear mushrooms in water for about half a day to reconstitute them. Cut off the hard stems. Soak the cellophane noodles in water for 15 to 20 minutes to soften.
2 Combine the mushrooms, noodles and the **Filling** ingredients in a bowl. Mix well until the meat is sticky.
3 Wrap the mixture with the softened rice paper (**see photos a-d**).
4 Fill a frying pan about two-thirds full with vegetable oil. Put in the rolls so they aren't touching one another (**e**). Turn the heat to medium, and fry the rolls slowly, turning them several times.
5 When the rice paper has turned hard, remove the rolls. Raise the temperature of the oil to 340°F (170°C) and put the rolls back in to crisp the surface. Arrange on a platter with the lettuce, herbs and nước chấm. Wrap the rolls in the lettuce leaves with the herbs, and eat while dipping in the nước chấm.

CHEF'S TIPS

The first recipe I learned to make in Vietnam was for these deep-fried spring rolls. We made so many, and there was such a huge mound of lettuce and herbs to go with them, that I couldn't believe at first that they'd all be eaten: but to my surprise, they were polished off. Eaten in the warm, humid climate of Vietnam, these piping-hot, crispy-on-the-outside rolls with their juicy fillings dipped in the sweet-sour sauce were so delicious. I made them again as soon as I got back home.

Breaded Seafood Spring Rolls Nem hải sản

Yumiko Adachi

Nem means "spring roll" in the northern Vietnamese dialect and hải sản means "seafood." This distinct style of breaded and deep-fried spring roll comes from Hanoi. It became very trendy in Vietnam about 15 years ago, and has since become a standard menu item. Crabmeat, red onions and coriander leaves/cilantro are mixed with mayonnaise, wrapped in rice paper, then breaded and deep fried until crispy.

Makes 8 rolls

8 square rice paper wrappers (page 19)
Vegetable oil, for deep frying

Filling
¼ cup (120 g) shredded crab meat
½ red onion, sliced thinly against the grain
⅔ cup (35 g) fresh coriander leaves/cilantro,
    chopped roughly
5 tablespoons mayonnaise
Black pepper

Breading
Cake or all-purpose flour
1 beaten egg
2 cups (225 g) breadcrumbs

Garlic Mayonnaise
6 tablespoons mayonnaise
½ grated garlic clove
1 teaspoon lemon juice

1 Mix the **Filling** ingredients together. Divide into 8 portions. Wrap each portion in a sheet of rice paper, fold in the sides and keep rolling to form tight spring rolls.
2 Coat the rolls in flour, egg and breadcrumbs, in that order.
3 Heat the oil to 340°F (170°C). Deep fry until golden brown.
4 Make the **Garlic Mayonnaise,** by combining the mayonnaise, garlic and lemon juice. Mix well. Serve with the spring rolls.

Crispy Stuffed Rice Paper Snacks Bánh tráng nướng
Masumi Suzuki

This is a classic food stall snack. Rice paper is topped with a meat-and-dried-seafood filling, and pan- or griddle-fried until crispy in this popular street snack. In the evenings, sellers pull out their portable cookers on the side of the street and cook these for you while you wait on plastic stools.

Serves 4

4 large round rice papers
4 eggs
12 tablespoons chopped green onions
8 to 10 small dried shrimp*
½ teaspoon shreds of dried squid*
Vietnamese chili sauce, to taste
(*Small dried shrimp and shredded dried squid are available at general Asian or Southeast Asian grocery stores.)

Filling
4 teaspoons sesame oil
1 garlic clove, chopped
8 oz (225 g) ground pork
1 teaspoon nước mắm
1 teaspoon seasoning sauce
1 teaspoon sugar
Black pepper

1 Make the **Filling**. Heat the sesame oil and garlic in a frying pan. When the garlic starts to become fragrant, add the ground pork and stir fry until it changes color. Add the rest of the ingredients and stir fry to combine the flavors with the meat.

2 Put the dry, unsoaked rice paper in a frying pan with a nonstick coating over high heat. When the frying pan is hot, lower the heat to medium.

3 Beat 2 of the eggs, and mix it with 6 tablespoons of the chopped green onions and half the meat mixture.

4 When the edges of the rice paper in the frying pan have started to curl up, put the meat-egg mixture from Step 3 on top (**photo a**) and spread it around evenly with a spoon (**b**). When the moisture from the egg has softened the rice paper, and the egg-meat mixture is drying out on top (**c**), sprinkle half the dried shrimp and squid evenly over it (**d**) and squeeze on some chili sauce (**e**). Fold the rice paper in half using a spatula (**f**). Repeat with the remaining rice paper and filling.

CHEF'S TIPS

There are an increasing number of sellers who top the rice paper with sausages, pizza cheese and shrimp too, but here I have recreated the flavors of original bánh tráng nướng. If you use cheap and brightly dyed dried shrimp instead of the more expensive, pale natural type, your snacks will more closely resemble the ones you can get from food stalls. The dried squid and the chili sauce are both quite salty, so don't season the meat too much.

Rice Paper & Green Mango Salad Bánh tráng trộn Shinobu Ito

This is another popular street snack. Rice paper strips, sauce, mangoes and tiny shrimp are put into a plastic bag and mixed. It's made to order in individual portions, mixed in a bowl and then put into a plastic bag, or just mixed up directly in the bag before it's handed to you. The rice paper gets soft and edible by absorbing the moisture from the sauce and the mango. Although it's eaten on its own as a snack in Vietnam, it's also great as an appetizer to enjoy with beer.

Serves 4

6 large round rice papers
3 tablespoons hot water
2 teaspoons sugar
2 tablespoons Vietnamese or Thai seasoning sauce
1 teaspoon vinegar
2 tablespoons fried onions
2 tablespoons chopped peanuts
2 lemon wedges

Filling
2½ cups (120 g) shredded green mango
(see Note 1)
2 batches Green Onion Oil, Version B (page 16)
6 tablespoons tiny dried shrimp
Freshly chopped coriander leaves/cilantro, to taste
Sate or Satay Sauce (see Note 2)

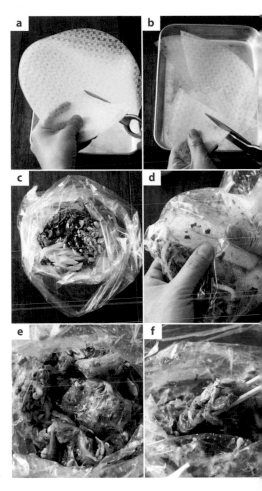

1 Cut the rice paper rounds in half with kitchen scissors (**photo a**), then cut into ¾-inch-wide (2-cm) strips (**b**).
2 Dissolve the sugar in the hot water. Combine with the seasoning sauce and vinegar to make the dipping sauce.
3 Put the half rice paper and a portion of the **Filling** in a plastic bag with 1 tablespoon of the Step 2 sauce. Mix well, taking care that the rice paper strips don't get stuck to one another.
4 When the rice paper and vegetables have wilted, add half the fried onions and peanuts and mix (**d**). Add more sauce to taste, and squeeze with lemon (**e**).

NOTE 1 If the green mango is too sour, sprinkle it with 1 to 2 tablespoons granulated sugar and rub it in with your hands. If you can't get green mango, substitute shredded carrot with 2 tablespoons each granulated sugar and lemon juice, rubbed in well.

NOTE 2 To make Sate or Satay Sauce: Put 2 finely chopped lemongrass stalks, 2 finely chopped garlic cloves and 6 tablespoons vegetable oil in a small pan and heat. When the garlic starts to change color, transfer the oil to a heatproof container and cool until lukewarm. Add 2 to 4 teaspoons chili powder and mix. (If you add the chili powder when the oil is hot, it will burn. Add it when the oil has cooled so the spiciness doesn't melt away.)

Fresh Spring Rolls Gỏi cuốn

Masumi Suzuki

Gỏi cuốn is a snack sold at food stalls across Vietnam, typically served with a miso-like bean paste sauce. The must-have fillings are shrimp, pork and lots of leafy vegetables and herbs. Recently, though, even in the South, where fresh spring rolls originate, some vendors have started serving a sauce made by mixing nước chấm with hot chili sauce, a delicious new twist.

Makes 6 rolls

6 medium shrimp
Salt
¼ lb (120 g) very thin slices of pork belly (see Note)
6 large round rice papers
6 perilla leaves or 12 mint leaves
1 small bunch thin green onions, cut into 4-inch (10-cm) pieces
1 small cucumber, deseeded and cut into strips
Daikon Radish and Carrot Marinated in Nước Chấm (page 17)
6 large leaves curly lettuce
Nước Chấm, Version C (page 16), hot chili sauce and sweet chili sauce, to serve with the spring rolls

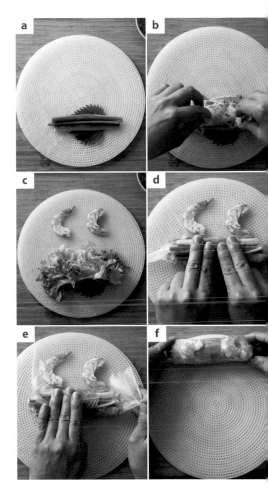

1 Bring a pan of water to a boil with a little salt added. Quickly blanch the shrimp, take them out, then boil the pork slices for a minute. Peel and clean the shrimp and cut in half lengthwise to make 2 thin pieces each.

2 Dip the rice paper in water and pat dry. On each rice paper, put 2 mint leaves, 3 scallion pieces, 2 to 3 cucumber pieces, 2 to 3 slices of pork, some of the marinated daikon radish and carrot and a palm-sized piece of curly lettuce on top. Place 2 pieces of shrimp on the far side of the rice paper (**photos a-c**). Soften the rice paper following the instructions on page 20.

3 Roll the rice paper tightly from the edge nearest you (**d**). Once you've rolled up to where the shrimp are, fold in both sides (**e**) and finish rolling up the rest (**f**). Repeat with the remaining rice paper and filling. Serve the rolls with nước chấm, hot chili sauce and/or sweet chili sauce for dipping.

> **NOTE** You can find very thinly sliced pork belly at Asian grocery stores. Otherwise, get a block of pork belly and freeze it for an hour, then slice it thinly with a sharp knife.

Chinese-Style Fresh Spring Rolls Bò bía (Popiah)

Shinobu Ito

Sausages, thin egg crêpes or omelettes and other ingredients are wrapped in rice paper to make these Chinese-style spring rolls. They are the original form of spring roll based on the gỏi cuốn, the fresh spring rolls we introduced you to on page 31.

8 rolls (Serves 4)

2 to 3 uncooked sweet Chinese sausages (lạp xưởng, see Note 1)
Vegetable oil, for frying
2 eggs
1 large pinch of salt
8 large round rice papers
4 to 5 leaves curly lettuce, ripped into bite-sized pieces
Bean spouts, trimmed, to taste
Thai basil and/or mint, fresh coriander leaves/cilantro, to taste

Shrimp Filling
4 tablespoons dried shrimp
1 tablespoon water
1 garlic clove, minced

Vegetable Filling
2 cups (3 oz) shredded cabbage
2 cups (3 oz) shredded carrot
1 large pinch of salt

Dipping Sauce
3 tablespoons hot water
2 tablespoons tianmianjiang/ sweet bean sauce (see Note 2)
1 tablespoon smooth peanut butter
1 garlic clove, minced
3 tablespoons coconut milk
1 teaspoon sugar (see Note 2)
Crushed peanuts, to taste
Hot chili sauce, to taste

1 Cut the sausages into thin diagonal slices. Heat up some oil in a frying pan, and fry the sausage slices.

2 Beat the eggs and salt in a small bowl. Heat up some oil in a frying pan, and cook the egg into 4 to 5 thin omelettes or egg crêpes. Cool, and cut into fine shreds.

3 To make the **Shrimp Filling**, sprinkle the shrimp with water to soften. Heat up some oil in a frying pan with the garlic, and stir fry the softened shrimp.

4 To make the **Vegetable Filling**, heat up some oil in a frying pan and add the cabbage and carrots. Cover the frying pan with a lid, turn the heat down to low and steam-fry the cabbage and carrot until wilted. Remove the lid and turn up the heat to evaporate any excess moisture. Season with salt and take out of the pan to cool.

5 To make the **Dipping Sauce**, dissolve the tianmianjiang and peanut butter in the water. Heat up some oil in a frying pan and add the garli. When the oil is fragrant, add the dissolved tianmianjiang and peanut butter. When it's bubbling, add the coconut milk and sugar to taste. Remove from heat and let the sauce cool, then distribute into small individual sized plates. Add peanuts and hot chili sauce on top.

6 Wrap the fillings made in steps 1 to 4 in softened rice paper: Put the water-dipped rice paper in a single layer on a tray or large baking sheet, and put a portion of the Step 1 filling about an inch from the near edge. Top with the Step 2 filling (**photo a**). Add the curly lettuce pieces to the near side, and top with the Step 3 filling (**b**). Squeeze a handful of the bean sprouts (**c**) and place on top (**d**). The bean sprouts are squeezed to break them, so they don't poke through the rice paper. Put the herbs on top, along with the Step 3 filling. Turn the tray one quarter, and fold in both sides of the rice paper. Turn the tray back to its original position, and roll up tightly from the near side (**e-g**). If the rolls are too loose they may fall apart while eating. Serve on plates with the dipping sauce on the side.

NOTE 2 Tianmianjiang is a sweet fermented Chinese bean paste, available at Asian grocery stores. Different brands have different levels of sweetness, so add the sugar only if needed, and adjust the amount to taste.

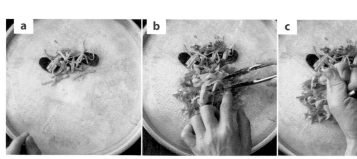

NOTE 1 Chinese sausage, called lạp xưởng in Vietnamese, is available at Asian grocery stores, where it's often sold frozen.

Raw Fish and Vegetable Spring Rolls Gỏi cá

Masumi Suzuki

Raw sashimi-grade fish, vegetables and herbs are mixed with a scrumptuous sauce and eaten wrapped in rice paper.

Serves 4

¼ fresh pineapple
1 small cucumber
10 leaves red leaf lettuce
Fresh coriander leaves/cilantro, to taste
½ lb (225 g) sashimi-grade red sea bream or similar white fish (such as red snapper)
20 square rice papers (page 19)

Fillings
1-inch (2.5-cm) piece ginger, peeled and finely shredded
4 sprigs dill
4 teaspoons peanuts
6–8 sprigs mint
¼ red onion, sliced thinly across the grain

Sauce
6 tablespoons Nước Chấm, Version C (page 16)
4 teaspoons hot chili sauce
4 teaspoons sesame oil

1 Peel the pineapple, and cut into matchsticks 4 inches by ½ inch long (10 cm x 1 cm). Slice the cucumber into thin, long ribbons using a vegetable peeler. Rip up the lettuce into palm-sized pieces. Cut the coriander/cilantro stalks into 4-inch-long (10-cm) pieces.
2 Slice the fish very thinly. Place the fish slices in the middle of a large plate, and put the **Fillings** around it. Roll the cucumber slices up, and arrange them with the pineapple and lettuce on a separate plate. Cut the rice paper in half, and serve arranged in a cup. Mix the **Sauce** ingredients together and serve in a small bowl.
3 Pour the sauce over the fish at the table (**photo a**), and mix all the ingredients on the plate together (**b**). Wrap this plus the other vegetables in rice paper to eat (**photos c-e**).

CHEF'S TIPS

Very thin, square rice paper is used here without presoaking, but if you have the thicker round ones, moisten them first. Add more sauce as needed when assembling the rolls at the table.

Deep-Fried Fish in Rice Paper

Cá chiên cuốn bánh tráng

Masumi Suzuki

The slowly fried fish is nutty and delicious. Arrange it so it looks like it's swimming.

Serves 4

1 whole blackhead sea bream or similar firm white fish, about 10 inches (25 cm) long
Vegetable oil, for deep frying
½ cucumber
⅛ fresh pineapple
Daikon radish (see cutting instructions)
4 thin scallions
Mustard greens (or arugula) and fresh coriander leaves/cilantro, to taste
2 oz (60 g) dried bún, soaked and boiled (page 45)
Daikon Radish and Carrot Marinated in Nước Chấm (page 17), as needed
Fresh mint and dill, to taste
12 square rice papers (page 19)

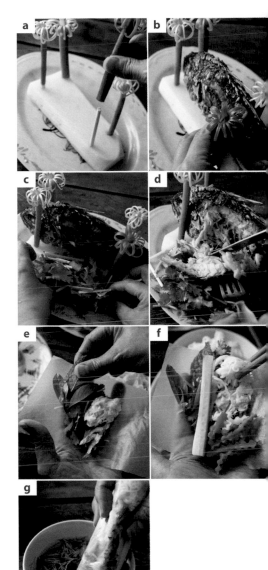

1 Put the whole cleaned fish into oil heated to 285°F (140°C), and raise the temperature to 340°F (170°C) while spooning the oil over the fish. Fry the fish for about 20 to 30 minutes in total.

2 Peel the cucumber and cut a piece that's 2½ to 3 inches (6 to 7 cm) long. Cut in half, remove the seeds and cut each half into 4 pieces. Core and peel the pineapple portion, and cut it into 2½- to 3-inch (6- to 7-cm) pieces. Cut the daikon radish into a 5-inch (13-cm) piece and peel. Split the scallions on one end only, using a water spinach cutter (see page 11), if you have one. Chop up the mustard greens (or arugula) and coriander leaves/cilantro roughly.

3 Pierce the daikon radish with 4 bamboo skewers. Insert the scallions with the skewers, so that the frayed ends face up (**photo a**). Push the fried fish from Step 1 between the skewers (**b**). Pile on the greens and cilantro/coriander leaves so the daikon radish is hidden (**c**). Serve the cucumber, pineapple, cooked bún, Daikon Radish and Carrot Marinated in Nước Chấm and mint on separate plates. Mix some fresh dill with nước chấm and serve on another plate. Cut the rice paper in half, and serve in a cup.

4 Flake the fried fish (**d**). To eat, take a piece of rice paper in your hand, top with any ingredients you like, and roll (**e-f**), dipped in the dill and nước chấm (**g**).

CHEF'S TIPS

Dab off the excess oil so the fish isn't too greasy. The skewers hold it perfectly in place for flaking.

Steamed Fish in Rice Paper Cá hấp cuốn bánh tráng
Masumi Suzuki

Steamed fish is a standard dish, eaten at home on special occasions and of course served in restaurants. It's eaten with bún sometimes too. Lemongrass-scented oil is poured over a plump and tender steamed fish.

Serves 4

1 whole sea bream
   or similar white fish
   (about 12 oz or 360 g)
1 stalk lemongrass
½ lemon
Salt, to taste
3 kaffir lime leaves
3 red chili peppers
About ¼ cup (60 ml) lúa
   mới (see Note)
Fresh vegetables and
   herbs (red leaf lettuce,
   mint, coriander leaves/
   cilantro, dill, Thai basil)
12 small round rice
   papers

Lemongrass Oil
1 stalk lemongrass,
   chopped
3 tablespoons
   canola oil

**Sauce (amounts are
   all to taste)**
Nước Chấm, Version
   C (page 16)
Fresh dilled,
   chopped
Fried onions
Black pepper
Green Onion Oil,
   Version C (page 16)

1 Clean the fish and remove the scales. Cut the lemongrass into 2-inch-long (5-cm) diagonal pieces. Peel the lemon and slice into rounds.
2 Place the fish on a deep heatproof dish, and sprinkle with salt. Top with the lemongrass, lemon, kaffir lime leaves and chili peppers. Pour in enough lúa mới to come up to about ⅓ inch (1 cm) of the dish.
3 Heat some water in a wok with a bamboo steamer placed on top. Put the dish in the steamer when the steam is rising. Cover with the lid, and steam for about 20 minutes.
4 Make the **Lemongrass Oil**. Put the chopped lemongrass and oil in a frying pan over medium-high heat. When the oil is fragrant and the lemongrass has browned, take the pan off the heat (**photo a**). Immediately pour it over the fish (**b**).
5 Flake the steamed fish (**c**). To eat, wrap some of the fish, lettuce and herbs on a softened rice paper (**d-e**) and dip in the **Sauce** (**f**).

CHEF'S TIPS

The flavors and sauces vary from place to place. Sometimes marinated vegetables are mixed into the sauce, or the fish is steamed with soy sauce. In the North, the fish is often combined with dill.

NOTE Lúa mới is a brand of Vietnamese distilled liquor made from medium-grain rice called rượu. If you can't find it, you can use sake or shochu instead.

NOTE Fermented tofu, also called fermented bean curd or soy cheese, is pungent, much different from regular tofu. It's sold in jars at general Asian or Chinese grocery stores.

Lamb with Fermented Tofu Sauce in Rice Paper

Thịt cừu nướng   Shinobu Ito

Succulent lamb is wrapped in rice paper and served with fermented tofu sauce on the side. The spicy marinated lamb dipped in the distinctively flavored fermented tofu sauce is a perfect marriage.

Serves 4

10 oz (300 g) thinly sliced lamb
7 oz (200 g) dried bún rice noodles
1 bunch spinach (about 7 oz/200 g)
Raw vegetables and herbs (lettuce, daikon radish, coriander leaves/cilantro, cucumber), to taste
10 stalks okra
2 Asian eggplants
Large round rice papers, as needed
Sate or Satay sauce (page 15)
Vegetable oil, for cooking

Seasoning

1 garlic clove, minced
1 piece ginger, minced
1 stalk lemongrass, minced
2 to 3 red shallots, minced
2 tablespoons Thai or Vietnamese seasoning sauce
1½ tablespoons sugar
2 tablespoons sesame oil
½ teaspoon turmeric powder
½ teaspoon five-spice powder

Sauce

2 tablespoons fermented tofu (see Note)
4 tablespoons water
3 to 4 tablespoons sugar
1 teaspoon sesame oil

CHEF'S TIPS

In Vietnam, goat meat is eaten regularly, and there are many variations of goat hot pots around the country. Goat hot pot restaurants also serve griddled or grilled goat, and people often have some grilled lamb before their hot pot. Lamb may be easier to get elsewhere, so I've used lamb here instead of goat, and adjusted the seasonings. You could also use beef.

1 Cut the lamb into bite-sized pieces. Combine the **Seasoning**, and mix with the lamb, rubbing it in well with your hands. Leave to marinate for about 15 minutes.
2 Put the fermented tofu from the **Sauce** ingredients in a bowl and mash into a smooth paste. Add the rest of the **Sauce** and mix. Divide onto individual plates.
3 Soak and boil the bún, and cut into easy-to-eat pieces (see page 45).
4 Cut up all the raw vegetables and herbs into easy-to-eat pieces, and arrange with the spinach on a plate.
5 Peel the tough calyx end of the okra, and cut in half lengthwise. Cut the calyx end off the eggplants and cut into ⅓-inch-thick (1-cm) slices. Arrange on a plate.
6 Cook the lamb with some oil on a griddle or in a frying pan. Cook the okra and eggplant on the same griddle or frying pan, mixing with the lamb marinade. Soak the rice paper in half and cut in half. To eat, wrap some of the raw and cooked vegetables and meat in the rice paper (**photos a-c**). Dip in the **Sauce**, adding some sate or satay sauce, to taste (**d**).

RICE NOODLES & MORE

The rice noodles most often eaten in Vietnam are bún, not phở!

Bún, Phở & Flat Rice Noodles

Bún

Made with fermented rice dough, which gives them their slippery texture, these are the noodles that say Vietnam. The dough is extruded, boiled and rinsed to make bún. Fresh noodles are available at markets throughout Vietnam. You may be able to find fresh bún at well-stocked Vietnamese grocery stores, but for most people dried bún is much easier to get at Asian grocery stores, online and some supermarkets. Dried bún is soaked in water before boiling.

Phở

The dough for making phở is made by soaking rice in water, grinding it up and adding more water to make it liquid. The mixture's then spread very thinly, steamed and cut into noodles. In Vietnam, fresh noodles are sold everywhere. You can find fresh phở at well-stocked Vietnamese grocery stores.

Dried phở, which has tapioca added to it to make it less brittle, is available at most Asian grocery stores, online and some supermarkets. Dried phở is soaked in cold water first, then put into hot water briefly before using.

Flat Rice Stick Noodles

There are several other kinds of rice and/or tapioca noodles in Vietnam, such as hủ tiếu and mì quảng. We've included recipes that use them, but if you can't find them you can use flat Thai rice stick noodles instead. Their names differ by how wide they are. Thick ones, about an inch (2.5 cm) wide, are called sen yai; medium-thick ones are sen lek; and the thinnest ones are called sen mee.

Shinobu Ito While phở is a relatively new noodle created during the French colonial period and eaten in specialty restaurants, bún is made at home. It's eaten in a variety of ways, mixed with vegetables like a salad, made into noodle soup, added to rice-paper-wrapped dishes and eaten with hot pots. Each region of Vietnam has different types of noodles, more than 10 types in total. Mì quảng (page 38) and Hủ tiếu (page 41) are regional dishes.

Yumiko Adachi One of the great things about Vietnamese cuisine is its wide variety of noodle dishes, including noodle soup, salad-like cold noodle dishes and the many types of noodles with sauce. Sometimes the same dish can be eaten in different ways, such as hủ tiếu (page 41), which can be a noodle soup or served with a sauce. I especially recommend the wide variety of mixed cold noodle dishes, such as bún thịt nướng and bún chả giò (both on page 32).

Masumi Suzuki Although phở and bún are generally only available in dried form outside Vietnam, in Vietnam it's sold in fresh form. My favorite Vietnamese noodle dish is phở. Northern Vietnamese-style phở is light and simply flavored, while southern-style phở is piled high with herbs and flavored according to the tastes of each diner. When choosing a good phở restaurant in Vietnam, aim for the ones where a ton of motorcycles are parked out front.

The Surprisingly Short History of Phở

Phở Was Born about 100 years ago

The Vietnamese noodle soup phở is popular worldwide, but just like spring rolls, it's not exactly a traditional Vietnamese dish that's been eaten for generations, tracing back about a century. Records indicate that bún, the nation's most popular noodle, was already being eaten in the 15th century, like soba and udon in Japan, noodles that have been eaten for hundreds of years. Phở, on the other hand, like ramen in Japan, is a fairly recent addition.

Phở Was Born During the French Colonial Period

Phở was first made in Nam Định province in northern Vietnam. There was a large textile factory there operated by the French. The original form of the dish was made by adding noodles to the stewed beef and vegetables eaten by the French living there. While water buffalo were eaten in Vietnam before the arrival of the French, beef was a novelty. The locals were amazed at how delicious it was. The French ate their stew with bread, but a version made with noodles to suit Vietnamese tastes is said to be the start of phở.

One theory for the origin of the word phở is that it came from feu (meaning "fire") part of the French home-cooked dish called pot au feu. Later on, a number of noodle makers surfaced in the village of Vân Cù in Nam Định province, which came to be called the "birthplace of phở." Making phở noodles became the major industry in the village, which has noodle factories larger than the ones in Hanoi.

Phở Becomes Established in Hanoi

After becoming established in Nam Định province, phở landed next in the city of Hanoi, also in the North. At the time, a type of noodle soup topped with stir-fried beef made by the Chinese immigrants in the city was popular. Phở soon appeared, and eventually became more highly regarded. Numerous phở shops sprang up in Hanoi, and the custom of eating beef likewise was firmly established.

Since there were two days out of the week when beef wasn't sold at the markets in Hanoi, some phở shops started using chicken instead. In later years phở was brought to the South by immigrants from the North. By the 1950s, phở became established in Hồ Chí Minh City too, cementing its reputation as a national dish.

Cooking and Presoaking Rice Noodles

All the rice noodles used in this book are soaked in plenty of cold or lukewarm water before boiling. If they're no longer hard or brittle when bent in half, they've been soaked enough. The soaking time and water temperature vary depending on the type of noodle. The times indicated here are general guidelines.

How to Cook Rice Vermicelli (Bún)

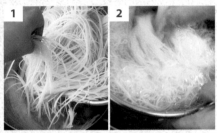

1 Separate the soaked noodles. Cook in boiling water for 1–2 minutes until cooked through yet not mushy.
2 Drain off the cooking water, put the noodles in cold water and rub them gently with your hands. Drain them again, and transfer to serving plates or bowls.

How to Cook Thick Phở Rice Noodles or Flat Noodles

1 Rinse the soaked noodles under running water.
2 Put one portion of noodles in a strainer with a handle. Dip the noodles in the strainer in a pot of boiling water for 20–30 seconds. When the noodles are limp, take them out right away.

3 Transfer to serving bowls or plates.

How to Serve Cooked Rice Vermicelli (Bún)

Bún is often served alongside hot pots, or wrapped with other fillings in rice paper. If you serve bún as is, the noodles will get stuck together, so it's a good idea to serve in small portions, depending on how they'll be eaten.

When serving them in a hot pot.
1 Cut the noodles into easy-to-eat lengths.
2 Use your fingers to wrap them into little nests.
3 Here's a ready-made example.
4 Serve it on a plate.

When serving them wrapped in rice paper.
1 Cut into short lengths.
2 Place the noodles in small 3-inch-long (8-cm) bundles on a tray or plate.

How to Cook Thin Flat Rice Stick Noodles

Put one portion of noodles in a strainer with a handle. Dip the noodles in the strainer in a pot of boiling water for 15 to 30 seconds to warm through. Drain well, and transfer to serving plates or bowls.

Soaking Times and Temperatures

Rice Vermicelli (Bún)

Cold water about 30 minutes

Thin Rice Stick Noodles (Phở)

Cold water about 1 hour or lukewarm water (body temperature) about 20 to 30 minutes

Thick Thai Rice Noodles or Flat Rice Noodles

Hot water (140–160°F or 60–70°C) about 15 to 20 minutes

Stir-Fried Cellophane Noodles with Crabmeat

Miến xào cua   Yumiko Adachi

The cellophane noodles soak up the delicious chicken broth and the umami of the crab meat. Serve with several generous grinds of black pepper on top to give the dish that extra zing.

Serves 4 to 6

8 oz (225 g) dried mung bean cellophane noodles
½ lb (225 g) crab meat
4 tablespoons vegetable oil
2 tablespoons minced garlic

3 cups (750 ml) chicken phở soup (page 36)
4 tablespoons nước mắm
4 tablespoons chopped green scallions
1 teaspoon black pepper
A few fresh sprigs of coriander leaves/cilantro

1 Cut the mung bean noodles into easy-to-eat pieces, and soak for 15 to 20 minutes in cold water. Pick over and shred the crab meat.
2 Heat the oil and garlic in a frying pan. When the oil is fragrant, add the crab and stir fry briefly. Remove from the pan.
3 Put the chicken soup in the frying pan and bring to a boil. Add the nước mắm, then the soaked and drained noodles, and stir so that the soup is absorbed into the noodles. When there's no moisture left in the pan, add the stir-fried crab from Step 2 back in.
4 Add the scallion and black pepper and mix. Transfer to serving plates, and top with the coriander leaves/cilantro sprigs.

Bún Noodles with Deep-Fried Spring Rolls

Bún chả giò   Yumiko Adachi

This is a mixed bún dish. Southern-style deep-fried spring rolls called chả giò are snipped in half with scissors and served on top of the bún.

Serves 4

5 oz (160 g) dried bún rice noodles
Vegetable oil for the bún
4 to 5 red looseleaf lettuce leaves, ripped into bite-sized pieces
16 mint leaves
¾ cup (75 g) bean sprouts, rinsed and trimmed
½ English cucumber, shredded
2 cups (100 g) Daikon Radish and Carrot Marinated in Nước Chấm (page 17)
16 to 20 chả giò deep-fried spring rolls (page 22), snipped in half with kitchen scissors
2 tablespoons chopped peanuts
Fresh coriander leaves/cilantro and mint, to taste
3 tablespoons per serving (12 tablespoons total) Nước Chấm, Version A (page 16)

1 Soak and cook the bún (see page 45), and cut into easy-to-eat pieces. Mix with some vegetable oil.
2 Arrange the lettuce, mint and bean sprouts on individual serving plates. Top with the bún. Add the cucumber, drained Daikon Radish and Carrot Marinated in Nước Chấm, halved spring rolls, peanuts, coriander leaves/cilantro and mint.
3 Spoon over the nước chấm. Mix well before eating.

Mixed Bún Noodles with Grilled Meat Bún thịt nướng   Yumiko Adachi

Lemongrass-scented marinated pork is browned and served on top of bún. Then it's all mixed together for a flavor combination that really pops.

Serves 4

10 oz (300 g) thinly sliced pork shoulder
5 oz (160 g) dried bún rice noodles
1 tablespoon vegetable oil, plus additional vegetable oil for the bún
2½ cups (120 g) Daikon Radish and Carrot Marinated in Nước Chấm (page 17)
½ cucumber, shredded
4 red looseleaf lettuce leaves
Mint leaves, to taste (or about ½ bunch)
2 tablespoons chopped peanuts

Marinade
2 tablespoons sugar
2 tablespoons nước mắm
2 tablespoons vegetable oil
3 tablespoons minced garlic
3 stalks lemongrass, chopped (about 6 tablespoons)
½ teaspoon ground black pepper

Sauce
¾ cup (180 ml) hot water
6 tablespoons sugar
4 tablespoons nước mắm
2 tablespoons lime juice
1 tablespoon minced garlic
2 red chili peppers

1 Slice the meat as thinly as possible (putting it in the freezer for an hour helps). Mix the **Marinade** and add the pork slices, rubbing it into the meat. Leave for 15 minutes.
2 Make the **Sauce**. Dissolve the sugar in the hot water, and combine with the rest of the sauce ingredients.
3 Soak and cook the bún (see page 45), and cut into easy-to-eat pieces. Mix with some vegetable oil.
4 Heat 1 tablespoon of vegetable oil in a frying pan, and panfry the marinated pork. When it's cooked through, flatten the pork with a spatula to give the surface a bit of a sear.
5 Arrange the bún on plates, and top with the pork, the drained Daikon Radish and Carrot Marinated in Nước Chấm, shredded cucumber, ripped-up lettuce, mint and peanuts. Add **Sauce** to taste, and mix before eating.

NOTE The pan-fried pork in this recipe is also delicious as an appetizer or as a bánh mì sandwich filling.

The rich, assertive flavor of the crab, ground to a paste, defines this quintessentially northern noodle soup.

Serves 4

1¼ lbs (300 g) frozen soft-shell crabs
2 teaspoons salt
4 tablespoons dried shrimp
5 to 6 scallions
2 medium tomatoes
2 tablespoons vegetable oil
10 oz (270 g) fried tofu
Vegetable oil, for deep frying
11 oz (320 g) dried bún rice noodles
Mint leaves, chiffonaded, to taste
Bean sprouts, to taste
Red chili peppers, sliced thin diagonally, to taste
Fermented shrimp paste (mắm tôm), to taste

Seasoning

2 tablespoons (or to taste) nước mắm
1 tablespoon rice vinegar
Salt, to taste
1 teaspoon sugar
2 teaspoons (or to taste) fermented shrimp paste (mắm tôm), see photo
Black pepper, to taste

1 Open up the defosted crab shells and remove the gills (**photo a**), and the shell on the underside too (**b**). Cut the crabs in half, and chop in a food processor (**c**).
2 Transfer the crab to a bowl, add 3½ cups (600 ml) water and mix well (**d**). Strain through a fine mesh sieve into a pan. Return what's left in the sieve to the bowl, add another 3½ cups (600 ml) of water and mix again. Strain this into the pan too.
3 Add the salt and the remaining water to the pan. Heat over low and slowly bring to a boil. When bits of crab are floating to the surface, turn the heat down very low and simmer for 2 to 3 minutes. Turn off the heat, skim off the crab on the surface with a slotted spoon and transfer to a sieve (**e**). Squeeze out every bit of liquid from the crab bits in the sieve into the pan (**f**).
4 Rinse the dried shrimp quickly, and cover with boiling water. Leave for 10 minutes to soak. Drain the shrimp, reserving the soaking liquid. Divide the scallions into green and white parts. Bash the white parts with the side of your knife to bring out the fragrance, and finely chop the green parts. Cut the tomato in half horizontally, de-seed and cut each half into 6 pieces.
5 Put the oil, soaked dried shrimp and the white parts of the scallions in a frying pan. Stir fry until the oil is fragrant, add the tomato and continue stir frying. Transfer the contents of the frying pan to the pan from Step 2 along with the shrimp soaking liquid. Bring the pan to a boil, lower the heat and skim off the surface. Simmer for about 10 minutes, and add the **Seasoning**.
6 Cut the tofu into bite-sized pieces. Fry in oil until crispy.
7 Soak and cook the bún (see page 45) cut into easy-to-eat pieces and arrange in individual serving bowls. Top with the ground-up crabmeat from Step 3, chopped scallions and the fried tofu, and ladle soup into the bowls. Serve with the mint, bean sprouts, chili peppers and mắm tôm on the side.

NOTE Mắm tôm is fermented shrimp paste (left). If you can't find it, you can substitute Chinese shrimp paste (top center) or the Thai shrimp paste called kapi.

Fried Fish and Dill Bún Noodle Soup Bún cá

Shinobu Ito

The bones of the fish are used to make the soup, and the fish itself is crisply fried to use as a topping for this refreshingly flavored tomato-and-dill noodle soup.

Serves 4

1 firm white fish such as sea bream (about 1¼ pounds/ 300 g)
2-inch (5-cm) piece ginger, sliced thinly
7 cups (800 ml) water, plus additional water
2 medium tomatoes
5 to 6 scallions
4 tablespoons vegetable oil
Rice flour or all-purpose flour
Vegetable oil, for deep frying
10 oz (325 g) dried bún rice noodles
¼ cup (60g) celery, roughly chopped
Fresh dill, to taste, roughly chopped
Black pepper, to taste
Green looseleaf lettuce, to taste, shredded roughly
Bean sprouts to taste, rinsed and trimmed

Seasoning
4 tablespoons nước mắm
2 teaspoon rice vinegar
1 teaspoon sugar
Salt, to taste

Marinade
1 teaspoon nước mắm
½ teaspoon sugar
Black pepper, to taste
1 teaspoon turmeric powder

1 Remove the scales from the fish and filet it (**photo a**). Cut the fish into thin diagonal slices (**b**). Put the bones (**c**) in boiling water briefly until it changes color (**d**), then drain and rinse under running water.

2 Put the rinsed fish bones, ginger and water in a pan and bring to a boil. Turn the heat down to low, and simmer for 15 to 20 minutes. Strain the broth through a fine mesh sieve, and add more water to bring it up to a little less than 12 cups (2.8 l).

3 Cut the tomatoes in half horizontally, remove the seeds and cut each half into 6 pieces. Divide the scallions into the white and green parts. Roughly chop the green parts, and bash the white parts flat with the side of your knife before chopping them finely.

4 Put the oil and the white parts of the scallions in a pan and stir fry. When the oil is fragrant, add the tomatoes and continue stir frying. Add the strained broth from Step 2, raise the heat to high and bring to a boil. Turn the heat down to low and skim the surface. Simmer for about 5 minutes, then add the **Seasoning**.

5 Mix the **Marinade** with the fish slices from Step 1 and let it marinate for 5 minutes. Coat with the rice or all-purpose flour. Deep fry in 340°F (170°C) oil until crispy, take it out once, and fry again for a couple of minutes to crisp and brown (**g**).

6 Soak and cook the bún (page 45), and put into individual serving bowls. Heat up the soup from Step 4, add the green parts of the scallions and celery. Turn off the heat. Pour the soup over the bún and top with the fried fish and some dill. Grind on some black pepper. Add the lettuce and bean sprouts, to taste.

CHEF'S TIPS

The delicate fish bones add lots of extra flavor here. Just be sure a stray one doesn't make into the finished dish.

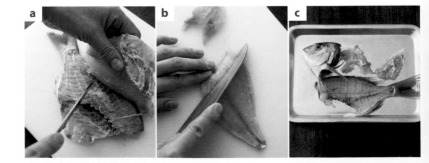

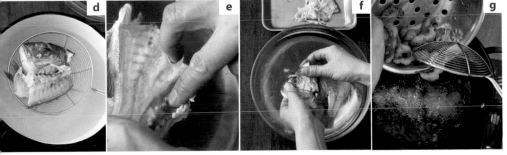

Chicken Phở Phở gà

Yumiko Adachi

This is a simple northern-style phở that's eaten with just scallions. It highlights the depth of flavor that can be achieved in a simple soup made from bone-in chicken. Store any leftover soup in the freezer in a plastic container.

Serves 4 (Makes about 7 cups or 1.75 l)

Soup
2¼ lbs (1000 g) bone-in chicken thighs
1 lb (450 g) boneless chicken breast
4 large knobs (120 g) ginger
2 leeks
6 quarts (6 l) water
8 to 10 thin scallions

7 cups (1.75 l) of the chicken soup above
9 oz (280 g) dried bún rice noodles
3 tablespoons nước mắm
4 teaspoons salt
Black pepper, additional salt, hot chili sauce, sliced red chili peppers and lime wedges, to taste

CHEF'S TIPS

For this easy-to-make yet deeply flavored soup, I've used bone-in chicken thighs and boneless chicken breast, and bashed the leek and ginger to bring out their flavor and fragrance. The bone-in chicken still has lots of flavor after making the soup, so you can add it to the phở, or serve it as a side dish or appetizer with some sauce and boiled chicken (page 95).

1 Make the **Soup**. Rinse the chicken well. Bash the ginger and leek with a rolling pin (**photo a**) to crush them. Put all the soup ingredients into a large pot with the water, and bring to a boil over high heat (**b**). When it comes to a boil, turn the heat down to low and simmer uncovered for 15 to 20 minutes, taking out the chicken breast halfway through when it's cooked through. (Store the chicken breast with a bit of the broth spooned over it (**c**) covered with plastic (**d**) until the phở is ready to serve.) When the bone-in chicken floats to the surface, simmer for another 10 minutes and turn the heat off. (Reserve the chicken thighs for the Lemongrass Chicken on page 95.) Strain the soup. You will have around 10 plus cups (2.4 l) of soup.

2 Cut the chicken breast into ¼-inch (5-mm) slices. Divide the green and white parts of the scallions, and chop the green parts finely. Cut the white parts into 3-inch (8-cm) pieces.

3 Soak the phở (see page 45).

4 Heat up 6½ cups (1.6 l) of the soup, and adjust the seasoning with nước mắm and salt. Add the white parts of the scallions from Step 2.

5 Briefly cook the phở in individual portions in boiling water and put into bowls (see page 45). Top with the sliced chicken breast, and sprinkle with black pepper. Serve with some hot chili sauce, red chili peppers and lime wedges on the side, and add, to taste, while eating.

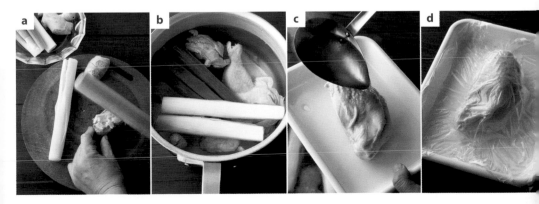

Chicken and Turmeric Soup with Wide Rice Noodles
Mì Quảng gà

Shinobu Ito

This is a regional noodle dish from Quang Nam province, and its main city of Hội An. This is a very hearty mixed-noodle dish with plenty of rich broth. Squeeze on some lemon for a refreshing pop of flavor.

Serves 4

12 oz (350 g) dried sen yai (wide Thai rice stick noodles, page 43)
1 lb (450 g) chicken wings—the middle and end sections only
7 to 8 chicken gizzards
1 medium tomato
4 tablespoons vegetable oil
2 garlic clove, minced
4 shallots, minced
1 teaspoon turmeric powder
1 teaspoon sweet paprika

2 cups (475 ml) water
½ onion, cut into thin wedges
4 hardboiled eggs
Fresh vegetables and herbs (looseleaf lettuce, bean sprouts, mint) to taste
Green parts of 4 scallions, chopped
Fresh coriander leaves/cilantro, chopped
Peanuts, chopped
Rice paper with sesame, crisped in a dry frying pan

Sauces and garnishes (nước mắm, lime wedges, green chili peppers), to taste

Marinade
1 tablespoon nước mắm
1 tablespoon sugar
½ teaspoon salt
Black pepper, to taste

Seasoning
5 to 6 tablespoons nước mắm
Black pepper, to taste
Salt to, taste
Sugar, to taste

1 Soak the sen yai (see page 45).
2 Cut the chicken wings into pieces at the joints (**photo a**), then cut the wing tips in half lengthwise (**b**). Cut the gizzards in half and remove the white sinewy parts (**c-d**), making a cut in the middle of each piece (**e**). Combine the wings and gizzards and coat with the **Marinade**. Leave for about 30 minutes.
3 Remove the seeds from the tomato and chop roughly.
4 Put the oil, garlic, ginger and shallots in a pan and stir fry. When the oil is fragrant, add the tomato and continue stir frying.
5 Add the chicken wings and gizzards from Step 2 with the marinade liquid to the pan.

Cook until the surface of the chicken changes color, then add the turmeric and paprika.
6 Add the water and the onion. When the liquid comes to a boil, turn the heat down to low and skim the surface. Simmer for 15 to 20 minutes. Add the boiled eggs and simmer for another 5 minutes, then add the **Seasoning**.
7 Cut up the fresh vegetables and herbs into easy-to-eat pieces and mix together. Arrange on a serving plate.
8 Cook the sen yai briefly in boiling water (see page 45) and put on individual serving plates. Pour the soup with all its contents onto the noodles, and top with the scallions, coriander leaves/cilantro and peanuts. Serve the vegetables and herbs from Step 7, with the crispy sesame rice paper and sauce on the side.

NOTE Cut the green chili peppers and stand them up against the edge of the bowl in the soup, to transfer their hotness to the broth.

CHEF'S TIPS

Two types of noodles are typically used—a yellow one and a white one—made in the same way as phở, but thicker and chewier. A variety of proteins can be used to make this dish, including beef, chicken, pork, shrimp, eel and other seafood. It's said that there are as many types of mì quảng as there are kitchens and restaurants. It's usually served at restaurants with the soup and ingredients separated, but here I've given you a homestyle version where they're all mixed together.

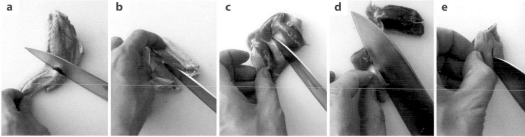

a   b   c   d   e

This is a new type of phở that has become popular recently in trend-conscious southern Vietnam. I think that new, fun dishes seem to spread around the country from the South. Pile high with fresh herbs when eating.

Serves 4

20 medium shrimp with the
  heads on
1 tablespoon minced garlic
1 tablespoon rice bran oil
4 cups (1 l) water
3 tablespoons nước mắm
1 teaspoon salt
10 oz (300 g) dried phở rice
  stick noodles
3 to 4 stalks scallions, chopped
½ shallot, thinly sliced
Fresh herbs (coriander leaves/
  cilantro, mint, Thai basil), to
  taste
Hot chili sauce and lime
  wedges, to taste

CHEF'S TIPS

The tasty hepatopancreas (the part that's also called the "tomalley" in lobster) inside the shrimp heads adds richness to the already well-flavored soup of this phở. Be sure to stir fry the shrimp heads very well to bring out their full flavor and give the soup a toasty, nutty fragrance.

1 Peel and clean the shrimp, leaving the tails on. Reserve the shrimp heads.
2 Heat the oil and garlic in a pan over medium. When the oil is fragrant, add the shrimp heads, and stir fry while crushing them with the spatula to extract the insides. Cook the shrimp heads through thoroughly.
3 When the shrimp heads are very fragrant and toasty and have turned a bright red, add the water to the pan. Bring to a boil, skim off the surface and season with nước mắm and salt.

Pass the broth through a strainer, and bring it back to a boil. Add the peeled shrimp from Step 1. When the shrimp are cooked, turn the heat off.
4 Soak the phở and pass briefly through boiling water; put into individual serving bowls (see page 45). Ladle on the soup and shrimp, and top with the chopped scallion and sliced shallot. Add fresh herbs and hot chili sauce, to taste, and squeeze on some lime juice before eating.

Clam Phở Phở nghêu

Masumi Suzuki

Phở used to be made with beef only, but this clam version is common these days in southern Vietnam. You can whip up a very rich broth in a short amount of time if you use shellfish.

Serves 4

1 tablespoon minced garlic
1 tablespoon canola oil
1¼ lbs (about 500 g) Manila clams, rinsed and scrubbed (page 113)
4 cups (1 l) water
3 tablespoon nước mắm
1 teaspoon salt
10 oz (300 g) dried phở rice stick noodles
3 to 4 stalks scallions, chopped
½ red onion, thinly sliced
Fresh herbs (coriander leaves/ cilantro, mint, Thai basil), to taste
Hot chili sauce and lime wedges, to taste

CHEF'S TIPS

This phở is packed with the umami of the clams. If you can't find Manila clams, use littleneck clams instead.

1 Put the garlic and oil in a pan and stir fry. When the oil is fragrant and the garlic lightly browned, add the clams.
2 When the clams are well-coated with oil, add the water. When they've opened up, season with nước mắm and salt.
3 Soak the phở and pass briefly through boiling water; put into individual serving bowls (see page 45). Ladle on the soup and clams, and top with the chopped scallion and sliced red onion. Add fresh herbs and hot chili sauce, to taste, and squeeze on some lime juice before eating.

Cambodian-Style Noodle Soup Hủ tiếu nước Nam Vang

Shinobu Ito

The broth is made by simmering pork, squid and dried shrimp. It's a hearty concoction, topped with pork liver, ground pork and shrimp.

Serves 4

8-inch (20-cm) piece dried squid (see Note)
8 cups (2 l) water
2 tablespoons dried shrimp
½ medium onion
½ lb (225 g) pork shoulder
¼ lb (160 g) lean ground pork
8 medium shrimp
2 tablespoons rice vinegar
½ lb (225 g) pork liver
9 oz (280 g) dried sen lek (medium-wide Thai rice stick noodles, page 43)
8 boiled quail eggs, or 4 small boiled chicken eggs cut into quarters
Chopped scallions, to taste
Fried onions, to taste
Black pepper, to taste
Fresh herbs (coriander leaves/ cilantro, mint, Thai basil), to taste
Limes or key limes (page 13), to taste
Red chili pepper, to taste

Seasoning

2 tablespoons nước mắm
2 teaspoons salt
2 teaspoons sugar

NOTE Dried squid and shrimp are available at Asian grocery stores in various forms.

1 Grill the dried squid briefly over a gas flame to soften and char it (**photo a**). Rinse quickly to remove the charred parts (**b**). Put the squid, dried shrimp and water in a large pan, and leave to soak overnight.

2 Grill the onion or roast in the oven until softened and lightly charred (**c**) to bring out the sweetness. Rinse quickly to remove the charred parts (**d**).

3 Put the onion in the pan from Step 1 along with the block of pork shoulder (**e**). Bring to a boil, turn the heat down to a simmer and skim off the surface. Simmer for 30 minutes. Take the pork out and slice thinly. This broth will be the soup.

4 Put the ground pork in a small pan, and add enough of the soup from Step 3 to cover. Bring to a boil, skim off the top and simmer over low heat briefly until the pork is cooked. Take the pan off the heat and leave until cool (**f**). Drain the meat in a fine mesh sieve held over the large pan to drain the soup back into it. Reserve the cooked ground pork.

5 Clean the shrimp. Put in a small pan with just enough water to cover, and boil briefly until cooked. Leave to cool in the cooking liquid. Peel the shrimp when cool, leaving the tails on.

6 Bring some water to a boil in a small pan and add 2 tablespoons vinegar and the pork liver. Take out the liver when it's cooked through, and rinse under running water to remove any surface sliminess (**h**). Pat dry and slice thinly.

7 Soak the noodles, and dip individual portions in a strainer into a pot of boiling water for 20–30 seconds. When the noodles are limp, take them out right away (see page 45). Put the noodles into individual serving bowls.

8 Strain 3 cups (750 ml) of the soup from Step 3 into a pan, and add the **Seasoning**. Pour the soup over the noodles in the bowls. Top with the boiled eggs, sliced pork shoulder, ground pork, shrimp and liver. Add the chopped scallion, fried onion and black pepper, and serve with the fresh herbs cut up into easy-to-eat pieces, lime and red chili pepper.

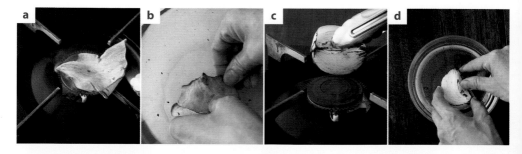

a b c d

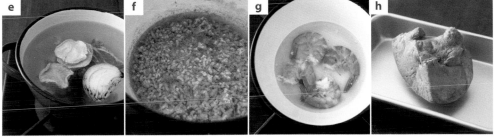

Cambodian-Style Mixed Noodles Hủ tiếu khô Nam Vang

Shinobu Ito

This is a mixed-noodle version of hủ tiếu made with the same ingredients as the similar soup featured on page 60. A sweet-salty sauce is mixed into the noodles after the toppings have been added.

Serves 4

9 oz (280 g) dried sen lek (medium-wide Thai rice stick noodles, page 43)

Pork shoulder, ground pork, shrimp, liver toppings (page 60)

Chopped scallions, to taste

Fried onions, to taste

Black pepper, to taste

Fresh herbs (coriander leaves/cilantro, mint, Thai basil), to taste

Limes or key limes (page 13), to taste

Red chili pepper, to taste

Seasonings

8 teaspoons Thai seasoning sauce

4 teaspoons sweet soy sauce (see Note)

4 teaspoons oyster sauce

4 teaspoons vegetable oil

4 teaspoons sugar

NOTE Thai sweet soy sauce (called see ew waan) is fairly easy to find, and is used here. The Hungry Boy brand is available at most Asian grocery stores.

1 Divide the **Seasonings** between the bowls and mix.

2 Soak the noodles, and dip individual portions in a strainer into a pot of boiling water for 20 to 30 seconds. When the noodles are limp, take them out right away (see page 45). Put the noodles into individual serving bowls (**photo a**).

3 Mix quickly (**b**). Pile the toppings (pork, shrimp and the rest) on top. Add the chopped scallion, fried onions and black pepper, and serve with the fresh herbs cut up into easy-to-eat pieces, lime and red chili pepper.

CHEF'S TIPS

The rice noodle called kway teow was introduced to Southeast Asia by Chinese emigrants from Chaozhou in northern Guandong province. In Vietnam it spread throughout the South and came to be called hủ tiếu or "river noodles." There are several noodle dishes that use hủ tiếu, with variations in the soup or sauce used. The ones included here are in the style of the dishes brought by Chinese immigrants who came from Cambodia, back when the city of Phnom Penh in Cambodia was called Nam Vang. At restaurants specializing in hủ tiếu dishes, you can enjoy both the soup and mixed-noodle versions.

a

b

BÁNH MÌ SANDWICHES

Bánh mì doesn't mean "sandwich" but "bread"—the essential ingredient needed to make a perfectly crafted sandwich.

Bread Used for Bánh Mì

The French-style rolls eaten in Vietnam are light and airy with thin, crispy crusts. In order to find as close to the real thing as possible, we recommend buying lightweight, frozen baguettes or crispy sub rolls that you can buy at the supermarket. Use the closest thing you can find. Heat up the bread in the oven until the crust is crispy, then add the filling and eat right away.

Yumiko Adachi The first time I went to Vietnam, I couldn't manage to find a bánh mì stall until the last day of my stay. When I mentioned that to the vendor at the Bến Thành Market in Hồ Chí Minh City, she told me that I could get one at the noodle shop next door. "Sandwiches at a noodle shop?" I thought, but popped over anyway, and sure enough, they had a stack of baguettes. I pointed to one, and they made me a bánh mì sandwich. Meatballs they called siu mai were smashed on a light, crispy roll, sprinkled with a little Vietnamese soy sauce. That was it, so simple! From this delicious introduction, I got to know the varied world of bánh mì, which is so much more than the well-known sandwiches known in the West, but includes the steamed bánh mì found on page 51.

Shinobu Ito My favorite bánh mì is made to order with a freshly fried egg. Fried eggs are called trứng ốp la; the last two words are said to originate from the French phrase oeufs au plat, or "eggs on a plate," so when you order a bánh mì with fried eggs, you can just ask for ốp la. In that scrumptous fried-egg bánh mì is a strong reminder that the sandwich, and the bread-eating culture it's traced to, are a legacy of the French colonial period.

Masumi Suzuki In Vietnam, food that goes well with plain white rice is also put between sliced light baguettes to make sandwiches. In Hanoi, streetside skewer stalls sell a flattened bread dipped in honey and grilled over charcoal called Bánh Mì Nướng (page 154), and medicinal chicken soup is often served with fried bread on the side.

The Ever-Evolving Bánh Mì Sandwich

Yumiko Adachi

A World-Famous Treat

It's been about 20 years since I had my first bánh mì. Things sure have changed since then. Now you can pick up bánh mì at sandwich shops and restaurants throughout Japan, France, the United States, Canada and Australia, the countries where Vietnamese people primarily emigrated. In Vietnam, baguettes are served with stewed meat and vegetables, dipped into noodle soups, eaten with stir fries to sop up the sauce or nibbled as a drinking appetizer. The

bread is also steamed, topped with meat sauce and eaten wrapped in leafy vegetables or served as a snack with ice cream sandwiched in it.

What Is a Traditional Bánh Mì?

The pork liver paté bánh mì is perhaps the most basic. Ham hocks, steamed ground pork, shredded chicken or pork and meatballs are also traditional bánh mì fillings. They're usually topped with a sprinkling of Vietnamese soy sauce called nước tương (page 8), which is the same as Thai seasoning sauce. Marinated shredded vegetables, scallions, coriander leaves/cilantro and other fresh herbs or hot chili sauce are then added for you too. At breakfast time, a lot of bánh mì stalls or shops make a sandwich out of a freshly cooked omelette. In the South, griddled or panfried beef, crispy salt pork or stewed offal are popular fillings too. Most of these are sold by establishments that specialize in one type of bánh mì only, though new types of bánh mì are being continuously developed in Vietnam and around the world.

While there are still lots of stores or stalls that sell traditional, "old school" bánh mìs, the next wave of reinvented bánh mì—and the shops that sell them—have arrived. Chic wrapping papers, delivery-only bánh mì sellers as well as national chains are just some of the recent developments. Bánh mì made with a type of thin, long bread that is the speciality of the northern port city of Hai Phong also became trendy nationwide, and pressed hot sandwich bánh mì stalls have cropped up too. There seems a new type of bánh mì to discover every time I visit.

BÁNH MÌ THỊT
Vietnamese Barguette w Sliced Po

Dill-and-Tomato Omelette Bánh Mì

Bánh mì trứng chiên cà chua thì là   Yumiko Adachi

Omelettes are a standard bánh mì filling. This version has tomato and dill in it for a refreshingly tangy flavor.

Serves 4

4 eggs
1 medium tomato, deseeded and
    chopped roughly
¾ cup (10 g) fresh dill, chopped
3 tablespoons vegetable oil
4 half baguettes, each about 8
    inches (20 cm) long
4 tablespoons butter
4 oz (120 g) Marinated Daikon
    Radish and Carrot (page 17)
Hot chili sauce, to taste
Black pepper, to taste
Coriander leaves/cilantro, to taste

Seasoning
2 teaspoons nước mắm
1 teaspoon sugar
Pinch of black pepper

1 Break the eggs into a bowl and beat well. Add the **Seasoning** plus the dill and tomato, and mix well.
2 Heat the oil in a small frying pan. Add the egg mixture and swirl around the pan. When it has started to set, flip it over using a plate or lid held over the pan and cook the other side. Cool and cut into 8 wedges.
3 Heat up the baguettes, and cut them from the side almost all the way through. Spread the cut surface with butter. Put 2 of the omelette wedges in each baguette. Add the well-drained marinated vegetables, and sprinkle with hot chili sauce and black pepper. Then add the chopped coriander leaves/cilantro.

Lemongrass Beef Bánh Mì Bánh mì thịt bò nướng sả Masumi Suzuki

On the streets of Ho Chi Minh City, there are bánh mì stalls selling skewered beef or meatballs grilled over charcoal. They're one of my favorites, so whenever I see a vendor, I can't resist. Beef marinated in a lemongrass sauce is wrapped around even more lemongrass for added flavor and fragrance, then panfried or seared on a griddle.

Serves 4

5 to 6 lemongrass stalks
1 lb (450 g) beef chuck
4 crusty rolls, about 6 inches (13 cm) long
7 oz (200 g) unsalted butter, thinly sliced

Spread
½ teaspoon minced garlic
⅛ cup (20 g) minced red onion
1 tablespoon minced lemongrass
2 teaspoons nước mắm
1 teaspoon sugar
2 teaspoons oyster sauce
1 teaspoon sesame oil

Filling
Daikon Radish and Carrot Marinated in Nước Chấm
 (page 17), to taste
Chopped cucumber and mint, to taste
Thai seasoning sauce, to taste
Hot chili sauce, to taste

1 Cut the tough root ends off the lemongrass stalks (**photo a**). Peel a layer off the remaining stalks (**b**).
2 Combine the **Spread** ingredients and marinate the beef for 20 minutes in the sauce. Wrap the marinated beef around the prepared lemongrass stalks from Step 1 (**c**) and squeeze tightly (**d-e**).
3 Put the beef and lemongrass rolls in a nonstick frying pan over medium heat and fry, while turning, until browned.
4 To eat, split the rolls in half, toast them, then put butter on one half and the **Spread** on the other. Put the beef and **Filling** between the roll halves and enjoy (**f-g**).

CHEF'S TIPS

Here I've used thinly sliced beef, but I also recommend trying it with ground pork or mixed ground beef and pork. In that case, combine the Spread with the ground meat, and form it into a long stick around a lemongrass stalk. Then panfry it as with the thinly sliced beef version.

Fried Pork Cutlet Bánh Mì
Bánh mì thịt chiên xù

Masumi Suzuki

I came up with this recipe as a Vietnamese-flavored version of the fried pork cutlet sandwich that's a staple in Japan. I learned how to make this tasty cutlet when I was studying in Hawaii, at a cooking class there. It's great with plain rice and is perfect with a beer or cocktail. The pork is marinated in a sauce that contains fresh coriander leaves/cilantro, then it's coated in a breading with black sesame and deep fried.

Serves 4

16 thin slices pork shoulder
   (1 lb/500 g total)
Flour
Beaten egg
Black sesame seeds
Dry breadcrumbs
Vegetable oil, for deep frying
4 half baguettes, about 7 inches (15
   cm) long
Mayonnaise
Thinly sliced cucumber
Daikon Radish and Carrot Marinated
   in Nước Chấm (page 17)
Coriander leaves/cilantro, to taste
Mint leaves, to taste
Hot chili sauce, to taste

Marinade
2 tablespoons minced garlic
8 tablespoons minced red onion
8 tablespoons minced fresh
   coriander leaves/cilantro
8 teaspoon nước mắm
2 teaspoons sugar
1 teaspoon salt
1 teaspoon black pepper

1 Combine the **Marinade** and spread on both sides of the pork slices. Leave to marinate for 20 minutes.
2 Coat the pork in flour, beaten egg and black sesame seeds combined with the breadcrumbs, in that order. Deep fry in 340°F (170°C) oil.
3 Make a cut into the side of the baguette almost all the way through, and spread both sides with mayonnaise. Stuff with the fried pork cutlets, cucumber, the well-drained marinated vegetables, coriander leaves/cilantro and mint. Finish it off with some hot chili sauce, to taste.

Chicken Liver Pâté Bánh Mì Bánh mì patê gà

Shinobu Ito

Chicken liver pâté is a classic filling for bánh mì. Mix it well before spreading it on the bread for a creamy texture.

Serves 4

Chicken Liver Pâté—(see recipe below)—use ½ the amount

7 to 8 tablespoons salted butter

Two 14-inch (35-cm) baguettes, cut in half in the middle

½ cucumber, cut in half, de-seeded and sliced thinly

Southern Vietnamese-Style Pickles (page 17)

8 scallions, green parts only

Coriander leaves/cilantro, chopped roughly

Thai seasoning sauce, to taste

Black pepper, to taste

1 Bring the chicken pâté to room temperature, and mix well until it's fluffy (**photo a** below). Mix the butter until it's soft.

2 Toast the baguette until it's crunchy. Cut in half, and cut from the side into each piece almost all the way through.

3 Spread butter on both sides of the bread. Spread the liver pâté on one side.

4 Stuff in the cucumber, the well-drained marinated vegetables and coriander leaves/cilantro. Sprinkle with seasoning sauce and black pepper.

CHEF'S TIPS

The liver pâté used as a filling by bánh mì stalls and shops in Vietnam is made with pork liver, pork meat and back fat, but homemade pâté is often made with chicken livers, which are more expensive but easier to deal with. If you combine chicken livers with chicken meat, the pâté will be even lighter tasting. For this recipe, I've combined the chicken livers with pork for more flavor, and instead of a combination of pork meat and back fat, I've used pork belly, which is easier to find. There's less fat than when back fat is used, but the flavor is just as pronounced. Choose pork belly that's about half fat and half meat. This bánh mì is also delicious with red chili peppers or hot chili sauce added.

Chicken Liver Pâté Patê gan gà

Makes enough for 8 chicken liver pâté bánh mì

½ lb (225 g) chicken livers

1 tablespoon salted butter

1 garlic clove, minced

⅔ cup (100 g) minced onion

1 tablespoon brandy

½ lb (225 g) thinly sliced pork belly, roughly chopped

½ egg, beaten

Seasoning

1 teaspoon nước mắm

1 teaspoon salt

1 teaspoon sugar

½ teaspoon black pepper

A pinch ground nutmeg

1 Slice the chicken livers in half. Soak in a bowl of cold water, then drain and pat dry.

2 Heat a frying pan and melt half the butter. Add the garlic and stir fry. When it's fragrant, add the onion and stir fry until wilted. Remove from the frying pan and cool.

3 Melt the rest of the butter, add half the liver and saute briefly until browned on the surface over high heat. Sprinkle with the brandy (**b**) and cook briefly until the alcohol has evaporated. Take the liver out of the pan to cool.

4 Put the uncooked liver and

pork belly in a food processor (c) and process. When the mixture has become a light fluffy paste (d), add the cooked liver, beaten egg and the **Seasoning**, and continue processing until smooth (e).
5 Butter a terrine mold or similar container and put in the Step 4 mixture, smoothing out the surface. Cover with aluminum foil. Heat up some water in a wok with a bamboo steamer placed on top. Put the mold in the steamer when the steam is rising. Cover, and steam for about 20 to 30 minutes. When the juices run clear when pierced in the middle with a skewer, it's done (g). Take out the container, and leave to cool still covered with the foil. When it has cooled to room temperature, refrigerate for at least 3 hours.

Fried Fish Cake Bánh Mì
Bánh mì chả cá

Yumiko Adachi

The filling for this bánh mì is a light fish cake made with ground-up whitefish and dill. The surface is crispy and the insides are springy and delicious.

Serves 4

Vegetable oil, for deep frying
4 half baguettes, each about 8 inches (20 cm) long
4 heaping tablespoons butter
2½ cups (120 g) Pickled Green Papaya and Carrot (page 17)
Thai seasoning sauce, to taste
Black pepper, to taste
Coriander leaves/cilantro, to taste
Red chili peppers, sliced, to taste

Fish Cakes
½ lb (250 g) whitefish, ground in a food processor until smooth)
¾ cup (10 g) dill, roughly chopped
4 scallions, white parts only
1-inch (2.5-cm) piece ginger, minced
½ tablespoon sake
½ teaspoon black pepper
1½ tablespoons cornstarch

1 Make the **Fish Cakes**. Put the ingredients in a bowl and mix well. Divide into 4 portions, and form into patties with oiled hands. Heat a generous amount of oil in a frying pan, and fry the cakes (**photo a**).
2 Drain the oil, and cut the fish cakes into ⅓-inch (1-cm) strips.
3 Heat up the baguettes, and cut them from the side almost all the way through. Spread with butter. Put the fish cake strips in each baguette. Add the well-drained marinated vegetables, and sprinkle with seasoning sauce and black pepper. Add the coriander leaves/cilantro and chili pepper, to taste.

Tamarind Chicken Bánh Mì Bánh mì gà sốt me

Shinobu Ito

The sweet-sour tamarind sauce tastes great on the chicken. It's combined with crispy onion slices for a refreshing flavor.

Serves 4

1 lb (450 g) chicken thighs, poached
2 teaspoons nước mắm
Generous pinch black pepper
½ cup (120 g) tamarind paste
½ cup (120 ml) hot water
½ medium onion, sliced thinly
6 tablespoons salted butter
4 tablespoons vegetable oil
2 garlic cloves, minced
2 baguettes, approximately 14 inches (35 cm) long, cut in half
Coriander leaves/cilantro, roughly chopped
Hot chili sauce, to taste

Sauce
8 tablespoons sugar (see Note)
2 tablespoons ketchup
4 teaspoons nước mắm

CHEF'S TIPS

This is my take on a bánh mì filling made by stir frying chicken, crab and shrimp in tamarind sauce. I used to serve it at the café I worked at when I lived in Vietnam.

NOTE Adjust the amount of sugar depending on how tart the tamarind is.

1 Shred the poached chicken into thick finger-width strips, and sprinkle with the nước mắm and black pepper.
2 Soak the tamarind paste in the hot water to soften. When it's cooled, break the paste apart with your hands, and pass it through a sieve to remove the seeds and turn it into a smooth paste. Put the sliced onion into a bowl of water, and drain very well. Bring the butter to room temperature and mix well to soften.
3 Heat the oil and garlic in a frying pan. When it's fragrant, add the chicken and stir fry it. Take the chicken out of the pan.
4 Add the tamarind paste from Step 2 to the pan, and heat through until it's thickened. Add the **Sauce**. Put the chicken back in the pan and coat well with the sauce.
5 Make a cut into the side of the baguette almost all the way through, and spread both sides with butter. Stuff with the chicken, sliced onion and coriander leaves/cilantro. Sprinkle with hot chili sauce, to taste.

Steamed Bánh Mì Wrappers Bánh mì hấp

Yumiko Adachi

This dish was devised as a way to eat stale baguettes. It's usually made at home as a snack eaten for breakfast or any time of the day. Steamed slices of baguette are combined with shrimp, ground meat, shredded marinated vegetables and herbs, and eaten wrapped in leafy vegetables.

Serves 4

5 or 6 medium-sized shrimp (100 g), peeled
2 tablespoons vegetable oil
2 garlic cloves, minced
⅓ lb (150 g) ground pork
1 full or 2 half baguettes
2 tablespoons Green Onion Oil (page 16)
Red looseleaf lettuce, to taste
Fresh herbs (coriander leaves/ cilantro, mint, Thai basil), to taste
Pickled Green Papaya and Carrot (page 17), to taste
Chopped peanuts, to taste
2 tablespoons cornstarch
4 teaspoons water

Seasoning
2½ teaspoons sugar
2 teaspoons Thai seasoning sauce
Black pepper, to taste

Sauce
6 tablespoons sugar
¾ cups (180 ml) water
4 tablespoons nước mắm
1½ tablespoons minced garlic
Minced red chili pepper, to taste

1 Chop up the shrimp finely. Heat the oil in a frying pan and stir fry the garlic. When the oil is fragrant, add the ground pork and shrimp, and stir fry until the meat changes color. Add the **Seasoning** and mix. Combine the constarch with water and add to the pan to thicken the sauce. Transfer the mixture to a serving bowl, and sprinkle with peanuts.

2 Mix the **Sauce** ingredients together, and transfer to individual serving plates. Cut up the herbs into bite-sized pieces, and put on a serving platter.

3 Cut the baguette into ½- to ¾-inch (1¼- to 2-cm) slices. Heat up some water in a wok with a bamboo steamer placed on top, and put the baguettes in the steamer once the steam is rising. Steam for 5 minutes (**photo a**). When the bread is soft take it out of the steamer, brush with the green onion oil and put on a serving plate.

4 To eat, top a leaf of lettuce with some of the bread and the meat-shrimp mix (**b**). Add herbs and the marinated vegetables, form into a roll and dip into the sauce.

Chicken Curry with Bánh Mì
Bánh mì cà ri
Masumi Suzuki

In Vietnam, curry is made with sweet potatoes. The curry sauce, containing coconut milk, is thin and sweet and is designed to be eaten with bánh mì bread that you dip in the curry to absorb the flavors.

Serves 4

10 oz (300 g) boneless chicken thighs
8 oz (250 g) sweet potato, about (see Note)
Vegetable oil, for deep frying
2 tablespoons canola oil
2 tablespoons minced lemongrass
¼ cup (40 g) minced red onion
½ medium onion, sliced
Red chili pepper, minced, to taste
4 crusty rolls, or half baguettes, each about 6 inches (13 cm) long

Chicken Seasoning
1 tablespoon curry powder
½ teaspoon salt
1 tablespoon minced garlic
¼ cup (40 g) minced red onion

Curry Sauce
3½ cups (800 ml) coconut milk
1⅔ cups (400 ml) water
2 tablespoons curry powder
3 bay leaves
2½ tablespoons nước mắm
2 tablespoons sugar

Lime Sauce
Salt, to taste
Black pepper, to taste
4 tablespoons lime juice

1 Cut the chicken into bite-sized pieces. Rub the **Chicken Seasoning** into the pieces, and let marinate for 15 minutes.
2 Cut the sweet potato up roughly, and put into a bowl of cold water. Drain. Heat the oil to 320°F (160°C) and deep fry the sweet potato until cooked through.
3 In a frying pan, heat the canola oil, add the lemongrass and minced onion and stir fry. When it's fragrant, add the chicken from Step 1 and stir fry.
4 When the chicken has changed color, add the **Curry Sauce**. Simmer over medium heat.
5 When the chicken is cooked through, add the sweet potato and sliced onion. Simmer briefly, so that the onion is still crispy. Transfer to a bowl and serve with the bread.
6 Make the **Lime Sauce** by mixing the ingredients together in a small bowl at the table (**photo a**) and squeezing in lime juice (**b**).
7 Add minced red chili pepper to the lime sauce, to taste. Dip the bread in the curry and lime sauce to eat (**c**).

CHEF'S TIPS

This is a dish from the South. Coconut milk is used in the curry, much like in Thai curries. In Vietnam, curries are usually eaten with bread or bún, rarely with rice. Deep fry the sweet potato until it's tender on the inside and crispy on the outside, and don't overcook the onion, making sure it's still slightly crunchy. The chicken is dipped in the lime sauce as you eat it. Try squeezing more lime juice into the curry for a refreshing flavor. If you prefer it spicier, add lots of coarsely ground black pepper and chopped chili peppers.

NOTE Any kind of sweet potato is fine, as there are more choices available these days. Use the traditional orange ones or seek out the ones that have pale, creamy insides and purple-brown skins.

RICE FLOUR DISHES

Vietnamese rice flour, made with Indica rice, is transformed into a range of traditional treats.

The Rice Flour Used in Vietnam

In this book we've used Indica-based Vietnamese rice flour, but if you can't find that, you can often locate Thai or Chinese (or Taiwanese) rice flour instead. Just don't buy sweet rice flour by mistake. The one shown here is Thai rice flour.

Bánh Cuốn, a Northern Speciality

Of the nation's many rice flour dishes, bánh cuốn is perhaps the best known. Made of a thin, crêpelike rice-flour wrapper or skin that's steamed and stuffed with stir-fried ground pork and other fillings, it's served with a sweet-sour sauce made with nước mắm, citrus juice, sugar and red chili peppers. In southern and central Vietnam, it may be identified on menus as "steamed spring rolls."

Thanh Trì's Bánh Cuốn Is the Best

When I was training in Vietnam, I used to eat the bánh cuốn from the northern village of Thanh Trì a lot. The wrapper is thin and tender, the fried onions on top are crispy and fragrant, and the filling was simply ground pork with wood ear mushrooms. I still can't forget how delicious it was. The skins are key to a good bánh cuốn. In Thanh Trì, an heirloom variety of rice called gạo chiêm, which has big, round grains, is used. They're soaked for about 3 hours, ground into a paste with a grindstone and mixed with water and salt to make the skins. The skins are then prepared in a specialized steamer with no lid, so the pot's covered with a tightly stretched piece of fabric. The dough for the skin is rapidly and thinly spread on the fabric and steamed. The sauce served with bánh cuốn is as delicious as the main component. The recipe is a closely guarded secret of the village apparently, and no one would teach it to me. In Thanh Trì, they start making bánh cuốn at 2 every morning. By 4 or 5, about 200 of the village women each stack up and load 20 to 45 pounds (about 10 to 20 kilos) of bánh cuốn for the hour and a half drive to Hanoi to sell them.

Shinobu Ito Central Vietnam, and its anchor city of Hue, has an especially extensive range of rice flour dishes. The rice flour is cooked in different ways—steamed, panfried, grilled or deep fried—and by varying the size and thickness of the dough and the ingredients mixed in, each dish comes out different with its own distinct texture. Rice-flour dishes in Vietnam are similar to the dim sum of China: eaten as snacks in the morning, late at night or as a light bite during the day.

Yumiko Adachi My favorite rice-flour dish is the North's bánh đúc nóng. A loose, sticky rice dough is made by mixing rice flour as it's heated. This tasty treat is served with soup, ground meat and fried tofu. It has a uniquely thick and sticky texture.

Masumi Suzuki Rice flour is indispensable to Vietnamese cooking. Mixed with water and steamed, it becomes Bánh Bèo (page 82) or Bánh Cuốn Nóng, steamed spring rolls (page 86); add turmeric powder and panfry it to make Bánh Xèo (pages 88 and 90); or combine it with bananas and steam it to make Bánh Chuối, banana cake (page 134). Use rice flour, instead of wheat flour, to coat chicken or shrimp before deep frying. It's hard to guess how a lot of rice flour dishes will taste from the way they look. Bột Chiên (page 84) is made by cooking mochi cakes made with rice flour, cutting them and panfrying them, then cooking them in beaten egg. I still remember how amazed I was when I first saw how it was made. I love the sticky, gooey texture of rice-flour dishes, and the fresh spring rolls I serve at my restaurant are made with bánh bèo as wrappers.

Steamed Rice Cakes with Shrimp Flakes Bánh bèo   Masumi Suzuki

Rice-flour batter is steamed on a small plate, topped with a sweet-salty shrimp sauce and flaked shrimp: slippery and delicious! This is a dish from Hue. It can be served as it is here, on small plates, or taken off the plates before serving. The sauce is also Hue-style, salty and sweet. You can use crispy croutons instead of the pork rinds.

Makes 10

Green Onion Oil (page 16; use the entire batch)
Pork rinds, crushed
Coriander leaves/cilantro, to taste
Red chili peppers, minced, to taste

Sauce (see Note)
½ tablespoon canola oil
1 teaspoon minced garlic
6 shrimp heads
3½ tablespoons water
3 tablespoons nước mắm
3 tablespoons sugar

Shrimp Flakes
6 medium-sized fresh shrimp, shells on
A little sake
A pinch of salt

Batter
⅓ cup (50 g) rice flour
1 cup (210 ml) water
2 to 3 pinches of salt

> **NOTE** You can use 3½ table-spoons Shrimp Phở (page 58) mixed with 3 tablespoons granulated sugar instead.

1 Make the **Sauce:** Put the oil and garlic in a pan over medium heat. When the oil is fragrant, add the shrimp heads, and stir fry them while crushing them to extract the contents.
2 When the shrimp heads smell toasty and have turned bright red, add the water. Bring to a boil, skim off the surface and bring back to a boil. Add the nước mắm and sugar.
3 Make the **Shrimp Flakes:** Clean the shrimp while leaving the shells on. Add the salt, sake and shrimp to the hot water, bring to a boil and turn off the heat.
4 When the shrimp have cooled, peel and chop finely in a food processor. Put the chopped shrimp in a dry (no oil added) frying pan (**photo a**), and cook while stirring until it's dry and powdery (**b**). Make the **Batter:** Combine the rice flour and water and add the salt. Put some water in a wok with a bamboo steamer placed on top. Put 10 small heatproof plates in the steamer and turn on the heat. When the steam is rising, pour the batter onto the plates (**c**). Cover the steamer and steam for 4 to 5 minutes.
5 If the batter puffs up as soon as the steamer lid is taken off and then deflates again, it's cooked. If that doesn't happen, steam for another 1 to 2 minutes. Leave to cool down to room temperature.
6 Brush the steamed batter with green onion oil, put 2 teaspoons each of the shrimp flakes on each plate, and top with the crushed pork rinds and chopped coriander leaves/cilantro. Add sauce with chili peppers to taste. Peel off the batter from the plate with a small spoon to eat (**d**).

Fried Rice Cake with Egg Bột chiên

Shinobu Ito

Rice flour is steamed to make a mochi-like dough, cut into cubes then deep fried. The cake is combined with scrambled egg and served with shredded marinated vegetables.

Serves 4

2 cups (280 g) Indica rice flour (or Thai rice flour)
2 tablespoons cornstarch
½ teaspoon salt
1 cup plus 2 tablespoons (200 ml) cold water
2½ cups (600 ml) boiling hot water
1 cup (100 g) shredded green papaya (or daikon radish)
1 cup (100 g) shredded carrot

8 tablespoons vegetable oil
4 beaten eggs
5 to 6 scallions, chopped
Hot chili sauce, to taste

Seasoning
4 tablespoons hot water
2 tablespoon sugar
6 tablespoons Thai seasoning sauce
1 tablespoon rice vinegar

1 Put the rice flour, cornstarch and salt in a bowl and add the cold water. Mix well. Add the boiling hot water little by little while mixing (**photo a**). Transfer to a small, oiled baking dish (**b**). The batter may be thicker depending on the temperature of the water you add.

2 Heat some water in a wok with a bamboo steamer placed on top. Put the square container with the rice dough in the steamer when the steam is rising. Cover with the lid, and steam for about 15 minutes.

3 Take the baking dish out of the steamer and leave to cool. Take the dough out of the container. Spread a little oil on a knife and cut the rice dough into approximately 1-inch (2.5-cm) squares (**c**).

4 Put the shredded green papaya and carrot into a bowl of cold water to crisp up. Drain well.

5 Dissolve the sugar in the hot water, and mix with the other **Seasoning** to make the sauce.

6 Heat 2 tablespoons of oil in a frying pan, add the rice dough cubes from Step 3 and panfry slowly. Push the cubes that have turned crispy to the side (**d**). When all the cubes have become crispy, pour the beaten egg into the empty part of the frying pan and stir (**e**) to make scrambled eggs. When the eggs have started to set, add the scallion and mix it in with a spatula, covering the rice dough cubes with the egg (**f**). Transfer to a serving plate, and serve with the sauce on the side.

CHEF'S TIPS

Bột chiên is a Chinese dish that normally includes daikon radish. In Vietnam, the daikon radish is omitted when making these rice dough cakes. This is sold at food stalls cooked on big griddles.

Southern-Style Bánh Xèo Pancakes Bánh xèo miền Nam   Shinobu Ito

Bánh xèo is eaten in the southern and central regions of the country. The ones made in the central parts tend to be small, eaten with vegetables dipped in a sauce or wrapped in rice paper with vegetables. There are many kinds of dipping sauces too. The key to good bánh xèo is to shallow-fry the pancakes in plenty of oil. Them be sure to drain off the oil well.

Makes 5 to 6 pancakes

5 to 6 medium-sized shrimp
¼ lb (125 g) chopped roast pork
½ small onion
Vegetable oil, for frying
2 cups (250 g) bean sprouts
5 or 6 green or red lettuce leaves
Mint leaves, to taste
Coriander leaves/cilantro, to taste

Batter
⅔ cup (70 g) Indica rice flour (or
   Thai rice flour, see Note)
2 tablespoons cornstarch
½ teaspoon turmeric powder
¼ cup plus 1 tsp (70 ml) coconut
   milk
½ cup (120 ml) water
2 scallions, chopped

Sauce
¼ cup (30 g) shredded daikon
   radish
¼ cup (30 g) shredded carrot
½ teaspoon salt
6 tablespoons hot water
2 tablespoons sugar
2 tablespoons nước mắm
1 tablespoon rice vinegar
1 clove garlic, minced
Red chili pepper, minced, to taste

NOTE You can use a commercial bánh xèo mix instead of the rice flour and cornstarch. If the mix already contains turmeric, you don't need to add any more.

1 Make the **Batter**. Put the rice flour, cornstarch and turmeric powder in a bowl and mix together. Add the coconut milk, water and scallions and mix well.

2 Make the **Sauce**. Rub the salt into the daikon radish and carrot, and leave for 2 to 3 minutes. When the shredded vegetables have wilted, rinse well while rubbing under water to remove the salt. Squeeze out the excess moisture.
Dissolve the sugar in the hot water. Add the nước mắm, rice vinegar, garlic and chili pepper and mix well. Add the daikon radish and carrot. Divide onto individual plates.

3 Peel the shrimp, then cut in half lengthwise. Cut the pork into bite-sized pieces. Heat 1 tablespoon of oil in a frying pan. Stir fry the shrimp and pork, then remove from the pan. Cut the onion into wedges, separating each layer.

4 Heat a little vegetable oil in a nonstick frying pan, and swirl it around. When the oil has coated the entire surface of the pan, wipe it out with a paper towel (**photo a**).

5 Mix the batter again and put ⅓ to ½ of it in the heated oiled frying pan. Swirl it around so that it coats the bottom of the pan (**b**).

6 Lower the heat, and put the shrimp and pork from Step 3 and some bean sprouts on half of the pancake (**c**). Cover the pan with a lid and steam-cook for about 30 seconds.

7 When the bean sprouts have started to sweat (**d**), take the lid off and pour in 2 tablespoons of vegetable oil under the pancake from the edge of the pan (**e**). Don't spread the oil all around; just fry the part where you've added the oil, so that about ¼ to ⅓ of the pancake is fried. Repeat the process of adding oil and frying the pancake 3 to 4 times to fry the whole pancake little by little.

8 When the pancake is crispy, fold it in half with a spatula (**f**), then pick it up. Tilt the pancake over a tray lined with paper towels, and drain off the excess oil while holding onto the pancake with a pair of cooking chopsticks (**g**) or a small pair of tongs. Transfer to a serving plate with the sauce and cut-up vegetables and herbs. Cut the bánh xèo into easy-to-eat pieces with 2 spoons (**h**). To eat, wrap the pieces with the lettuce and herbs, and dip into the sauce.

CHEF'S TIPS

In Vietnam the pancake is made in a shallow aluminum or iron wok, but here I've used a nonstick frying pan, which is easier. The key to making bánh xèo is to fry it in plenty of oil until very crispy. If you're stingy with the oil, the pancakes will become heavy and greasy. The reason why the frying pan is oiled before the pancake is added is to fill in any scratches on the surface; otherwise the batter will get stuck to the pan. The oil is then wiped off the pan before adding the batter, so it will spread properly.

Central-Style Bánh Xèo Pancakes
Bánh xèo miền Trung
Shinobu Ito

Central style bánh xèo is made small, and dipped into a rich, thick meat sauce to eat.

Serves 4 (makes 8)

1 cup (100 g) shredded green papaya (or daikon radish)
1 cup (100 g) shredded carrot
2 tablespoons rice vinegar
2 tablespoons sugar
½ lb (250 g) medium shrimp
½ lb (250 g) thinly sliced beef
Vegetable oil, for frying
1 lb (500 g) bean sprouts
4 eggs, beaten
Rice papers softened in water (page 19)
Green or red lettuce, mint leaves, coriander leaves/cilantro and sliced cucumber, to taste

Batter
1¾ cups (180 g) rice flour (or Thai rice flour)
8 tablespoons cake flour or all-purpose flour
1 tablespoon turmeric powder
2 cups plus 1 tablespoon (500 ml) water

Sauce
2 tablespoons vegetable oil
2 garlic cloves, minced
¼ lb (125 g) lean ground pork
¼ lb (125 g) pork or chicken liver, chopped
2 cups (400 ml) water
6 tablespoons miso
2 tablespoons sugar (see Note)
½ cup (60 g) peanuts, chopped
4 tablespoons ground white sesame seeds
Cornstarch dissolved in water

1 Make the **Batter**. Mix the rice flour, sifted flour, turmeric powder and salt in a bowl. Add the water and mix well.

2 Make the **Sauce**. Put the vegetable oil and garlic in a pan and heat until the oil is fragrant. Add the ground pork and chopped liver and stir fry. When the meat is cooked, add the water and bring to a boil. Lower the heat and skim off the surface. Simmer over low heat to cook the meat and liver thoroughly. Add the miso, sugar, peanuts and sesame seeds, and thicken the sauce with the cornstarch dissolved in water. Cool, then transfer to individual serving plates.

3 Combine the green papaya and carrots. Sprinkle with the rice vinegar and sugar, and leave to marinate for about 30 minutes. When the vegetables have wilted, squeeze them lightly to remove excess moisture.

4 If the shrimp have thick shells, peel them; if they're thin-shelled, leave them on. Cut the beef into bite-sized pieces. Heat 2 tablespoons of vegetable oil in a frying pan and stir fry the shrimp and beef.

5 Heat 1 tablespoon of vegetable oil in a small frying pan, and then wipe out the excess oil from the pan (**photo a**). Mix up the batter again and pour it into the frying pan (**b**), spreading it around. Add ⅛ of the Step 4 shrimp and beef and ⅛ of the bean sprouts on top, and pour on ⅛ of the beaten egg. Cover with a lid and steam-cook over low heat.

6 When the bean sprouts start to sweat, take the lid off and pour in 2 to 3 tablespoons of vegetable oil under the pancake from the edge of the pan. Fry the pancake until it's crispy on the underside, and fold in half with a spatula.

7 Tilt the pancake over a tray lined with paper towels, and drain off the excess oil while holding the pancake on the spatula with a pair of cooking chopsticks (**c**) or a small pair of tongs. Transfer to a serving plate with the sauce and cut-up vegetables and herbs. Cut up the bánh xèo into easy-to-eat pieces with 2 spoons (**d**). To eat, wrap the pieces with the lettuce and herbs in rice paper (**e-f**), and dip into the sauce.

CHEF'S TIPS

This recipe is one that's popular in central cities like Da Nang and Hội An. The bánh xèo is wrapped in rice paper with herbs and vegetables and dipped in a meaty miso-based sauce.

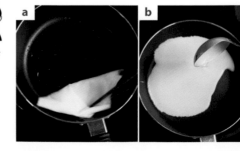

> **NOTE** Adjust the amount of sugar depending on how salty the miso is. The sauce should be strongly salty-sweet.

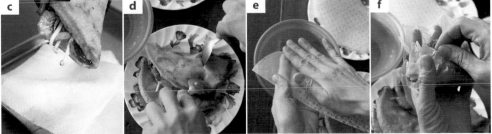

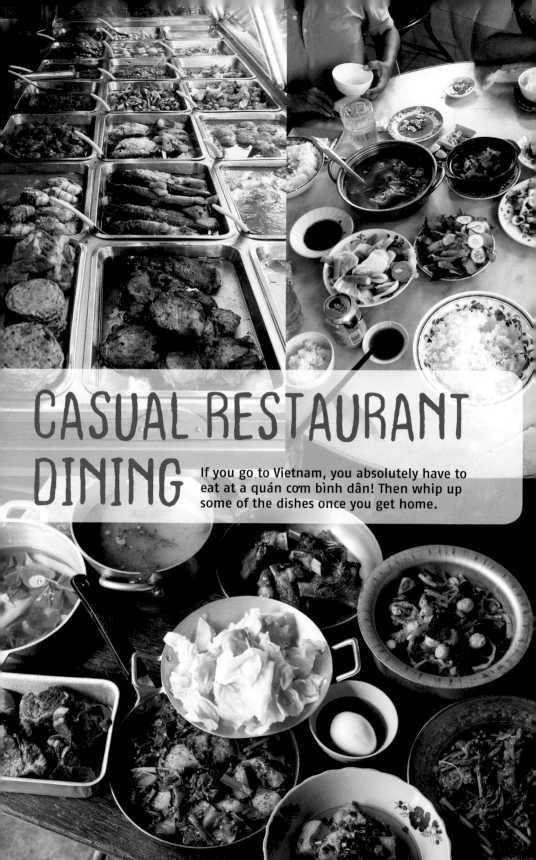

CASUAL RESTAURANT DINING

If you go to Vietnam, you absolutely have to eat at a quán cơm bình dân! Then whip up some of the dishes once you get home.

How to Eat at a Quán Cơm Bình Dân

A quán cơm bình dân is a simple working people's lunch place, where you get hearty, everyday food, and all the prepared dishes are on display. Here's how to eat at one in Vietnam.

1. Tell Them How Many Are in Your Group

It's a good sign of course if a place has a lot of motorbikes parked outside and is packed with customers inside. When you arrive, let them know how many people are in your group.

2. Point to the Dishes You Want

Order the dishes you want by pointing to them in the display case. Vietnamese people order a well-balanced meal of a meat or fish, vegetables and soup. Just follow your instincts and order whatever looks good!

3. Seat Yourself and Wait

After a short wait, your order will arrive on large platters and in basins.

4. Serve Yourself Some Rice and Top It with the Dishes You Ordered

Small rice bowls are brought to your table or are already stacked on the table. Fill one with rice, then top it Vietnamese-style, with the dishes you ordered.

5. Desserts Are Extra

Sometimes the desserts are already placed on the table, but these are an extra charge. The wet towels on your table are also extra, and you are charged by how many you use. After you've finished eating, call a server, point to your empty plates and show your wallet to indicate you want to pay your bill. It's helpful to have them write the amount on a piece of paper.

Shinobu Ito There are quán cơm bình dân all around Vietnam. Quán means "store," and cơm means "white rice." Here, quán cơm means "diner," and bình dân (pronounced bin zan) refers to an average Joe, an everyman. In this section, we introduce you to some typical quán cơm bình dân dishes, including soups, sides and mains, all collectively called cơm bình dân.

Yumiko Adachi Quán cơm bình dân always have beer, and I like to have some while munching on some appetizers. But it's always difficult to gauge when's the right time to start on the rice! Once I start eating rice, I can't drink beer anymore; its a dilemma.

Masumi Suzuki I love cơm bình dân so much, I often think that's what I'd like my last meal to be. The cơm bình dân in the North is not very sweet, while the offerings in the South are rich and sweet with sugar, coconut milk and coconut juice. I'm especially fond of going to quán cơm bình dân in the South that are run by folks from the North. There not only can you enjoy southern cooking, you can also find simmered pork, stewed green bananas with freshwater snails and other foods normally only found in the North.

Earthenware Pot Cooking: Home-Cooked Dishes Whose Flavors Differ by Region

Masumi Suzuki

Vietnam is very long from north to south, and the differences in regional cuisine similarly stretch far and wide. For instance, there's the simmered fish dish called Riềng (page 98). The basic method is to cook the pre-flavored fish in an earthenware pot (cá kho tộ) in a sweet-salty sauce with nước mắm, sugar, caramel sauce and aromatic herbs; but there are key differences between the various versions made in each of the major regions.

In the North, an abundance of aromatic herbs and vegetables like garlic, ginger, galangal (page 13) and lemongrass are used, and black pepper is sprinkled on to finish. The central region's sauce is very rich, the fish used quite oily, and pork belly and chili powder are added to the simmering liquid.

Coconut milk is the simmering liquid of choice in the South, and garlic and shallots (page 13) are used as aromatic vegetables. Plenty of black pepper and red chili pepper are added for spice. Whichever variation you prefer, the key to a delicious cá kho tộ is to use a top-class first-press nước mắm (page 8); it's great just on rice by itself!

Cơm Niêu Cooked in Earthenware Pots

One of my favorite Vietnamese rice dishes is cơm niêu. It's cooked with water in an earthenware pot in the oven. When it's done, the lid's removed and the pot is returned to the oven for the surface of the rice to turn brown and crispy. The thin, delicious crispy crust of cơm niêu is called cháy. Each grain of rice stands out on its own. Tan, an acquaintance of mine who's a master cơm niêu maker, shared his views: "The absolute best way to eat it is in a thatched hut, with everyone

sitting crosslegged on the dirt floor covered with a woven straw mat, in the flickering light of a lamp!" The traditional accompaniments for cơm niêu are the Rau Cần Xào Thịt Bò (page 105) and tép, as well as crushed peanuts mixed with salt (muối vừng).

Casual Recipes from the South Cơm bình dân miền Nam

Lemongrass Chicken Gà kho sả
Yumiko Adachi

The fragrance and subtle notes of the lemongrass are very refreshing in this well-flavored simmered dish. It's a perfect accompaniment to plain steamed rice.

Serves 4

2 tablespoons vegetable oil
1 tablespoon garlic, minced
2 tablespoons lemongrass, minced
1¼ lbs (600 g) boneless chicken thighs, cut into bite-sized pieces
¼ cup (60 ml) water
1 red chili pepper, cut into thin diagonal slices
Black pepper

Seasoning
2½ teaspoons sugar
2½ tablespoons nước mắm
½ teaspoon turmeric powder

1 Heat the oil in a frying pan and stir fry the garlic. When the oil is fragrant, add the lemongrass.
2 Add the chicken to the pan and stir fry until it changes color. Add the **Seasoning** and coat the chicken with it. Add the water and bring to a boil. Simmer over medium heat for about 15 minutes. When there's almost no liquid left in the pan, add the red chili pepper and black pepper.

Simmered Pork and Eggs Thịt kho trứng
Masumi Suzuki

A sweet-salty simmered dish of pork and eggs using coconut water.

Serves 4

¾ lb (325 g) pork shoulder
2 eggs
4 quail eggs (or use 1–2 more chicken's eggs)
½ teaspoon whole black peppercorns
1¼ cups (300 ml) coconut water
1 red chili pepper, sliced thinly diagonally

Marinade
1 clove minced garlic
8 tablespoons minced red onion
3 pinches black pepper
½ tablespoon nước mắm
1½ tablespoons sugar

1 Cut the pork into 1-inch (2.5-cm) cubes. Combine with the **Marinade** and leave for 15 to 20 minutes. Hard-boil the eggs.
2 Put the pork, eggs, peppercorns and coconut water in a pan and bring to a boil. Skim off the surface, turn the heat down to low and simmer for 20 to 30 minutes.
3 Add the red chili pepper, then mix and serve.

Yam Soup with Meatballs
Canh khoai từ nấu tôm thịt viên
Shinobu Ito

This is a soup thickened with sticky, viscous Chinese yam (called củ mài or khoai mài in Vietnamese), then topped off with hearty shrimp-and-pork meatballs.

Serves 4

3 to 4 scallions
2 tablespoons dried shrimp
6 shrimp (about 3½ oz/100 g),
  peeled and cleaned
2 oz (60 g) lean ground pork
1 tablespoon vegetable oil
3½ cups (800 ml) water
½ lb (250 g) yam or nagaimo
  (see Note)
Coriander leaves/cilantro,
  shredded, to taste
Black sesame seeds, to taste

Flavoring
1 teaspoon nước mắm
1 to 2 teaspoons cornstarch
A pinch of salt
A pinch of sugar
½ teaspoon black pepper

Seasoning
1 tablespoon nước mắm
Salt, to taste
A pinch of sugar

NOTE Chinese yam or nagai-mo is available at Asian grocery stores. If you can't find them, just use sweet potatoes from your local market.

1 Finely chop the green parts of the scallion. Bash the white parts with the side of your knife, then chop finely.
2 Rinse the dried shrimp quickly, and soak in hot water to cover for about 10 minutes. Drain the shrimp, reserving the soaking liquid. Chop up the shrimp roughly.
3 Line up the raw shrimp on a cutting board and cover with cling wrap. Bash the shrimp over the plastic wrap with a rolling pin, then chop it up.
4 Put the chopped shrimp and ground pork in a bowl and mix well until sticky. Add the chopped green scallion and the **Flavoring** and mix well. Form into small meatballs.
5 Put the vegetable oil and the dried shrimp from Step 2 in a pan and stir fry. When the oil is fragrant, add the shrimp soaking liquid and the water. Bring to a boil, and lower the heat to a simmer. Skim off the surface and cook for 7 to 8 minutes.
6 Add the meatballs to the soup. When the meatballs float to the surface, turn the heat off.
7 Peel the yams and grate. Add some of the soup to the grated yam to thin it out, then add the combined liquid back into the soup pan.
8 Heat the soup and add the **Seasoning**. Ladle into serving bowls and sprinkle with the remaining chopped scallions, shredded coriander leaves/cilantro and black pepper.

Sweet and Sour Shrimp Soup Canh chua tôm

Yumiko Adachi

Canh chua is great to have on a hot summer's day, when you don't want to eat much and just want something light and refreshing.

Serves 4

1 heaping tablespoon tamarind paste
½ cup plus 1 tablespoon (100 ml) hot water
½ cup plus 1 tablespoon (100 ml) cold water
1 tablespoon vegetable oil
1½ tablespoons minced garlic
8 medium shrimp
1 medium onion, cut into thin wedges
1½ cups (300 ml) water
Coriander leaves/cilantro, to taste
Red chili peppers, sliced into rounds, to taste
Garlic oil (see Note)

Fruit & Vegetables

3½ tablespoons sugar
1 teaspoon salt
¼ cup (80 g) sweet potatoes, peeled and cut into ¾-inch-wide (2-cm) slices
4 okra, cut in half diagonally
¼ pineapple (about 3½ oz/100 g), cut into bite-sized pieces
1 small tomato, cut into wedges

Sprouts & Seasoning

1 teaspoon nước mắm
Black pepper, to taste
½ cup (60 g) bean sprouts, trimmed

> **NOTE** To make garlic oil: Heat 2 tablespoons minced garlic and 6 tablespoons vegetable oil in a pan and mix. When the garlic starts to change color, take the pan off the heat and cool.

1 Soften the tamarind paste in the hot and cold water combined. Turn it into a paste, passing it through a sieve to remove the seeds.
2 Heat the oil in a frying pan and stir fry the garlic. When the oil is fragrant, add the shrimp and stir fry. When the shrimp changes color, add the onion and stir fry briefly.
3 Add the water and bring to a boil. Lower the heat and add the tamarind from Step 1.
4 Bring the pan back to a boil, skim off the surface and add the **Fruit & Vegetables** in the listed order. Simmer briefly.
5 Add the **Sprouts & Seasoning** and bring back to a boil. Turn off the heat.
6 Serve in bowls topped with coriander leaves/cilantro. Serve the red chili pepper and garlic oil on the side.

Braised Fish with Pork

Cá kho   Masumi Suzuki

Caramelized sugar and pork belly are added to this rich-tasting dish for a memorable marriage of flavors.

Serves 3

1 tablespoon sesame oil
¾ lb (350 g) firm oily fish fillets (such as mackerel), cut into pieces
¼ lb (125 g) pork belly, cut into ½-inch (1-cm) strips
1⅔ cups (400 ml) water
1½ tablespoons nước mắm
3 tablespoons sugar
¼ red onion, thinly sliced
1 large piece ginger, thinly sliced
1 teaspoon whole black peppercorns

1 Heat the sesame oil in a frying pan. Add the fish and brown on both sides.
2 Put the nước mắm and sugar in a small pan, and stir while cooking, until the sugar is caramelized, to make the caramel sauce.
3 Add the pork to the pan and stir fry quickly. Add the water.
4 Add the contents of the Step 3 pan to the Step 1 frying pan with the red onion, ginger and the peppercorns. Bring to a boil, skim off the surface and simmer over a low heat until the sauce is slightly thickened.

Stuffed Tofu with Tomatoes

Đậu hũ chiên sốt cà chua   Yumiko Adachi

Lemongrass-flavored pork is stuffed into thick fried tofu and simmered in a nước-mắm-flavored tomato sauce.

Serves 4 (8 pieces)

10 oz (300 g) fried tofu
Cornstarch
Vegetable oil
1 tablespoon minced garlic
Black pepper

Pork

1 lb (450 g) ground pork
1 tablespoon minced garlic
4 scallions, white parts only, minced
3 dried wood ear mushrooms (10 g), soaked for half a day in water, stems removed, minced
4 tablespoons minced lemongrass
1 teaspoon nước mắm
1 teaspoon sugar
1 teaspoon black pepper
½ teaspoon salt

Sauce

3 large tomatoes, chopped roughly
2 tablespoons nước mắm
2 tablespoons sugar
½ teaspoon salt

1 Cut the fried tofu in half, and cut each half into 2 triangles. Scoop out a little of the insides. Mix the scooped-out portion with the **Pork** ingredients.
2 Dust the insides of the fried tofu pieces, and stuff with the Step 1 mixture.
3 Fill a frying pan about one-third full with vegetable oil and heat. Fry the stuffed tofu, starting with the cut sides to firm them up. Then fry the other sides, turning the tofu pieces several times.
4 Take the tofu out of the oil. Add the garlic to the oil and stir fry. When the oil is fragrant, add the **Sauce** and simmer for about 10 minutes. Return the fried tofu to the pan, and simmer for another 10 minutes or so.
5 Serve with black pepper sprinkled on top.

Stir-Fried Okra and Tomato
Đậu bắp xào cà chua   Shinobu Ito

Blanch the okra briefly to retain its crispy texture. Then stir fry it quickly with the tomato.

Serves 4

½ lb (250 g) okra
Pinch of salt
2 small tomatoes
1 tablespoon dried shrimp
2 tablespoons vegetable oil
1 garlic clove, minced

Seasoning
1 tablespoon Thai seasoning sauce
1 teaspoon nước mắm
2 teaspoons sugar
Black pepper

1 Bring some water with a little salt added to a boil. Quickly blanch the okra for a few seconds, drain and cool in cold water. Drain again well. Peel off the ends, and cut the okra in half diagonally.
2 Cut the tomatoes into wedges.
3 Soak the dried shrimp in lukewarm water to cover for about 5 minutes. Drain and chop roughly.
4 Heat the oil in a frying pan and stir fry the garlic. When the oil is fragrant, add the shrimp and stir fry.
5 Add the tomatoes and stir fry quickly. When the tomatoes are heated through, add the okra, stir fry very briefly then add the **Seasoning** and serve.

Pork & Vegetable Soup
Canh rau tần ô thịt bằm   Yumiko Adachi

The umami of the ground pork and the bitterness of the greens are a great match. You can always substitute watercress, if you can't find chrysanthemum greens.

Serves 4

1 bunch chrysanthemum greens or
    watercress (approximately ¼ lb/120 g)
½ lb (250 g) ground pork
1 tablespoon vegetable oil
½ tablespoon minced garlic
3½ cups (800 ml) water
Salt and pepper, to taste

Marinade
½ teaspoon nước mắm
Black pepper

Seasoning
1½ tablespoons nước mắm
1 teaspoon sugar
½ teaspoon salt

1 Cut the root ends off the chrysanthemum greens or watercress, and chop up roughly.
2 Rub the **Marinade** into the ground pork to flavor it.
3 Heat the oil in a frying pan and stir fry the garlic. When the oil is fragrant, add the ground pork and stir fry until the color of the meat changes. Add the water and bring to a boil. Turn the heat down to low and skim off the surface. Add the **Seasoning** and the chrysanthemum greens or watercress. Serve in bowls and sprinkle with salt and pepper.

Grilled Eggplant with Pork Cà tím nướng thịt bằm

Shinobu Ito

A very hearty eggplant dish topped with onion oil and seasoned ground pork, this substantial side could easily mask as a main.

Serves 4

4 long medium Asian eggplants or 1 large globe eggplant
Green Onion Oil (page 16), the entire batch
1 tablespoon vegetable oil
1 garlic clove, minced
2 shallots, minced

Sauce
3 tablespoons hot water
1 tablespoon sugar
1 tablespoon nước mắm
1 tablespoon lemon juice
½ garlic clove, minced
Red chili pepper, minced, to taste

Seasoning
2 teaspoons nước mắm
Pinch of sugar
Pinch of black pepper

1 If using long Asian eggplants, grill them whole in the oven or on a stovetop grill pan, turning frequently, until soft; the skin will be charred. If using a large globe eggplant, cut it into quarters and grill until soft. Peel off the skin while still hot (hold it in a kitchen towel to protect your hands), and arrange the strips on a plate.

2 Make the **Sauce**. Dissolve the sugar in the hot water, and mix with the remaining ingredients.

3 Add the oil, garlic and shallots to a pan and stir fry. When it's fragrant, add the ground pork and stir fry until crumbly. Add the **Seasoning**.

4 Put the ground pork mixture on the eggplant pieces and pour the green onion oil over all. Serve with the sauce on the side, to pour over and mix while eating.

Steamed Egg with Spicy Pork Chả trứng

Masumi Suzuki

This hearty egg custard is steamed in bowls, with the savory addition of ground pork, cellophane noodles and wood ear mushrooms. Be sure to cook it through.

Makes 4

1 oz (25 g) dried mung-bean
   cellophane noodles
3 wood ear mushrooms
   (10 g), soaked in water for
   half a day until softened,
   stems removed, minced
6 eggs
Vegetable oil, for the pan
2 teaspoons sesame oil
4 red chili peppers
Coriander leaves/cilantro, to
   garnish

Pork
2 oz (50 g) ground pork
½ tablespoon minced ginger
¼ cup (100 g) minced red
   onion

Seasoning
4 teaspoons nước mắm
2 teaspoons sugar
½ teaspoon black pepper

**Four 4 x 1½ inch deep (10 x 4
   cm) bowls**

1 Soak the cellophane noodles in water until softened, and cut into ½-inch (1-cm) pieces.

2 Put the cellophane noodles, minced wood ear mushrooms and the **Pork** ingredients in a bowl and mix.

3 Break the eggs and reserve 4 of the yolks separately. Beat the remaining yolk and the 6 egg whites together with the Step 2 ingredients. Mix in the **Seasoning**.

4 Oil the insides of the bowls. Divide the Step 3 mixture between the 4 bowls. Heat some water in a wok with a bamboo steamer placed on top. Put the bowls in the steamer when the steam is rising. Cover with the lid, and steam over low heat for about 15 minutes.

5 Mix the 4 reserved egg yolks with sesame oil.

6 When the custards are cooked through (they should have puffed up a bit, and if you insert a bamboo skewer in the middle the liquid should run clear), take the bowls out of the steamer, and spread the Step 5 egg yolk mixture thinly over the top. Return the bowls to the steamer, and steam for 3 minutes with the lid on, and an additional minute with the lid off. When the egg yolk on the surface has firmed up and is glossy, the custards are done. Cool and top with the chili pepper and a light sprinkle of coriander leaves/cilantro.

Crispy Spareribs with Sweet Nước Mắm Sauce
Sườn rán chua ngọt
Yumiko Adachi

Spareribs are stewed until tender, then fried until crispy and served with a spicy hot sweet-sour vinegar sauce.

Serves 4

2 lbs (900 g) pork spareribs
Vegetable oil, for deep frying
6 tablespoons sugar
2 tablespoons water
Red chili pepper, chopped, to taste
Black pepper, to taste
8½ cups (2 l) water
The white part of a scallion (bash with the side of a knife)
1-inch (2.5-cm) piece ginger, unpeeled

Sauce
5 tablespoons nước mắm
2 tablespoons rice vinegar
½ tablespoon Thai seasoning sauce

1 Blanch the spareribs in boiling water for a few seconds until the surface changes color. Drain, and rinse the spareribs in cold water. Put the rinsed spareribs in another pan with the water, scallion and ginger and bring to a boil. Simmer over low heat for 40 to 50 minutes, skimming off the surface. Take the spareribs out and drain in a colander. Pat dry with paper towels.
2 Heat oil to 355°F (180°C). Deep fry the spare ribs until crispy.
3 Heat the sugar and water in a frying pan until melted. Add the **Sauce**. Simmer briefly, add the red chili pepper and black pepper, then coat the spareribs with the **Sauce**.

Cabbage with Boiled Egg and Nước Mắm Sauce

Bắp cải luộc chấm nước mắm dằm trứng   Masumi Suzuki

Boiled cabbage is dipped in a nước-mắm-based sauce with crushed boiled egg in it.

Serves 3 to 4

½ head cabbage

Sauce
2 tablespoons nước mắm
2 tablespoons water
3 pinches sugar
1 egg, hard-boiled

1 Cut up the cabbage into large pieces, and blanch briefly. Make sure not to overcook it, and that it still remains crispy.
2 Put the **Sauce** on a small plate. Mash up the boiled egg and mix well.
3 Dip the cabbage in the **Sauce** to eat.

Sweet Soy-Stewed Pork and Eggs Thịt kho xì dầu   Shinobu Ito

This is a simmered pork dish that uses Thai seasoning sauce while retaining its strong Chinese influence.

Serves 4

1 lb (450 g) pork shoulder or belly
Fried onions, to taste

Marinade
2 tablespoons Thai seasoning sauce
2 tablespoons raw cane sugar or light brown sugar
½ teaspoon black pepper
1-inch (2.5-cm) piece ginger, thinly sliced
2 shallots, thinly sliced

Sauce
1 tablespoon Thai seasoning sauce
2 tablespoons raw cane sugar or light brown sugar
2 tablespoons oyster sauce

1 Cut the pork into 2-inch (5-cm) cubes. Put into a pan, and coat with the **Marinade**. Let stand for about 30 minutes.
2 Turn the heat to medium. When the seasonings come to a boil, turn the pork to cook the surface, adjusting the heat so the seasonings don't burn.
3 When the seasoning liquids become very thick, add enough water to cover the pork and bring to a boil. Lower the heat, cover with a lid and simmer for about 30 minutes.
4 Poke several holes in the surface of the boiled eggs with a bamboo skewer. Put about ⅓ inch of oil into a small frying pan, heat over medium, put in the boiled eggs and fry while turning them. Drain off the oil.

5 Add the **Sauce** to the Step 3 pan and check the seasoning. Add the fried boiled eggs and simmer over medium heat for about 10 minutes, until the sauce is thickened. Serve with fried onions on top.

Clam, Tomato and Dill Soup
Canh hến thì là   Masumi Suzuki

The umami of the clams, the sourness of
the tomato, and the fragrance of the dill
are the features of this delicious soup.

Serves 4

1¼ lbs (about 550 g) small clams (see Note)
1-inch (2.5-cm) piece ginger, thinly sliced
4¼ cups (1 l) water
½ tablespoon vegetable oil
1 teaspoon minced garlic
2 tablespoons minced onion
1 medium tomato, cut into wedges
¾ cup (10 g) fresh dill, chopped up roughly

Seasoning
1⅓ tablespoons nước mắm
1 teaspoon salt
2 to 3 pinches of sugar

1 Soak, rinse and scrub the clams under
running water (page 113).
2 Put the clams, ginger and water in a pan and
bring to a boil. When the clams have opened
up, skim off the surface and turn off the heat.
Take the clams out and remove the insides from
the shells.
3 In a separate pan, stir fry the garlic and onion
in the oil until fragrant, then add the tomato
wedges and stir fry.
4 Put the clam broth and the clam meat into
the Step 3 pan and bring to a boil. Add the
Seasoning and the dill.

> **NOTE** Small clams are ideal for this dish but use
> any type you prefer.

Fried Tofu in Nước Mắm Sauce
Đậu phụ rán tẩm hành   Yumiko Adachi

Crispy fried tofu is dipped in a nước-
mắm-based sauce with scallions in it.

Serves 4

5 oz (150 g) fried tofu (see Note)
2 tablespoons chopped scallion
½ cup plus 1 tablespoon (100 ml) hot water
1 scant tablespoon nước mắm
1 tablespoon sugar
Red chili pepper, chopped, to taste
Vegetable oil, for frying

1 Cut the fried tofu into 8 pieces.
2 Put the scallion on a heatproof container, and
pour in the boiling hot water. Add the nước
mắm and sugar and mix to dissolve the sugar.
Add red chili pepper to taste.
3 Heat the oil to 340°F (170°C) and deep fry
the tofu until the surface is very crispy. Put the
freshly fried tofu in the Step 2 sauce, and leave
to let the sauce permeate the tofu.

> **NOTE** Use thick fried tofu, not the thin ones
> called tofu puffs or tofu skins.

Stir-Fried Beef and Celery
Rau cần xào thịt bò   Shinobu Ito

In this simple but satisfying stir fry, celery is combined with beef and tomato, and lightly seasoned.

Serves 4

¼ lb (100 g) thinly sliced beef
1 small bunch water spinach (available at Asian grocery stores) or 4 to 5 stalks celery
½ small tomato
2 tablespoons vegetable oil
1 garlic clove, minced
Coriander leaves/cilantro, roughly chopped, to taste

Seasoning 1
½ teaspoon nước mắm
1 pinch of sugar
A little black pepper

Seasoning 2
2 teaspoons nước mắm
½ teaspoon sugar
A little black pepper

1 Cut the beef into bite-sized pieces, and combine with **Seasoning 1**. Wash the water spinach and cut into lengths. If using celery, cut it into thin strips of 3-inch (8-cm) lengths. Cut the tomato into wedges.
2 Heat the oil in a frying pan and stir fry the garlic. When the oil is fragrant, add the beef and stir fry until the color changes. Add the tomato, and when the tomato skin starts to curl up, add the water spinach or celery, stir fry quickly and add **Seasoning 2**. Serve with coriander leaves/cilantro on top.

Northern-Style Crab Soup
Canh cua mồng tơi   Shinobu Ito

In Vietnam, this soup is made with a freshwater crab paste, but here I've used frozen softshell crabs instead.

Serves 4

1 lb (450 g) frozen soft-shell crab
¾ lb (350 g) malabar spinach (see Note)
6 cups (1.5 l) water
4 tablespoons sake
½ teaspoon salt, plus more, to taste
½ teaspoon sugar

1 Defrost the soft-shell crabs in the refrigerator. Rinse in cold water, and pat dry with paper towels. Remove the gills and the belly side of the shell. Chop up the rest roughly and pulse in a food processor until it turns into a paste (**photos a-c** on pages 50–51).
2 Divide the leaves from the stems of the malabar spinach or greens. Cut up both into bite-sized pieces.
3 Mix the crab paste from Step 1 with the water, and pass it through a sieve (**photo d** on page 51). Put the strained liquid in a pan, add the sake and salt and bring to a boil. When bits of crab come floating to the surface, lower the heat and simmer for 2 to 3 minutes.
4 When the crab meat is cooked, add the sugar and an additional pinch of salt and the spinach or greens. Simmer briefly before serving.

> **NOTE** Malabar spinach has purple stems. If you can't find it, substitute Swiss chard, mustard greens or regular spinach.

Chicken Soup with Lotus Root and Lotus Seeds
Gà hầm hạt sen

Shinobu Ito

The chicken is so tender, as are the lotus root and seeds in this delicious soup. If you can't find the seeds, substitute blanched almonds. Water chestnuts serve as a suitable replacement for the lotus root.

Serves 4

1½ cups (50 g) dried lotus
    seeds (available online or from
    Chinese/Asian grocery stores)
Boiling water for soaking the
    lotus seeds
3½ cups (800 ml) hot water
¾ lb (350 g) boneless chicken
    thighs
2 to 3 scallions, chopped roughly

Vegetables
½ lb (225 g) lotus root
5 to 6 dried wood ear
    mushrooms
1 teaspoon nước mắm
½ teaspoon sugar
A little black pepper
2 to 3 shallots, minced

Seasoning
1 tablespoon nước mắm
Salt, to taste
½ teaspoon sugar
A little black pepper

1 Bring water about 3 times the volume of the lotus seeds to a boil. Turn off the heat and add the lotus seeds. Cover with a lid, and soak overnight. Soak the wood ear mushrooms for half a day in water, remove the stems and cut into bite-sized pieces. Peel and slice the lotus root ¼-inch (5-mm) thick, and put the slices into a bowl of cold water.

2 Drain the lotus seeds. Add water to the pan, bring to a boil and add the lotus seeds back to the pan. Simmer over low heat until the seeds are tender: when you bite into one, it should have the texture of a roasted or boiled chestnut. Drain the seeds, keeping the cooking water. Add more water to the pan to make it 3½ cups (800 ml) in total.

3 Remove any fat from the chicken and reserve. Cut the chicken meat into ¾-inch (2-cm) cubes, and mix with the **Vegetables**.
4 Add the chicken fat to a wok or a pan for deep frying pan, and stir fry over low heat to melt the fat. (If there isn't enough fat, add some vegetable oil.)
5 Add the shallots to the pan and stir fry. When it's fragrant, put in the cubed chicken and stir fry until it changes color. Add the hot water from Step 2 and the drained lotus root slices, and bring to a boil. Simmer for about 20 minutes, until the lotus root is tender.
6 Put the lotus seeds and wood ear mushrooms in the pan and bring to a boil. Add the **Seasoning**. Add the chopped scallion, turn off the heat and serve.

Fried Fish with Pickled Mustard Greens and Tomatoes

Cá om dưa

Shinobu Ito

Crispy fried fish is quickly simmered in a sauce made with pickled mustard greens and tomatoes.

Serves 4

1 cup (150 g) Thai or Chinese pickled mustard greens (available at Asian grocery stores)
¾ lb (350 g) firm fish, such as mackerel or swordfish
3 to 4 scallions
1 medium tomato
Vegetable oil, for frying
1 garlic clove, minced
½ cup plus 1 tablespoon (100 ml) water
Fresh dill, roughly chopped, to taste
A little nước mắm
A little black pepper

Seasoning

1½ tablespoons nước mắm
½ teaspoon sugar
A little black pepper

1 Rinse the pickled mustard greens briefly, and cut into easy-to-eat pieces. Soak in plenty of cold water for 15 minutes to remove the excess salt. Drain and squeeze out tightly. Pat the fish dry with paper towels, and cut into bite-sized pieces. Combine with the nước mắm and black pepper and leave for about 10 minutes. Slice the green parts of the scallions, and finely chop the white parts. Cut the tomatoes in half horizontally, remove the seeds and cut each half into 6 pieces.

2 Add enough oil to a frying pan to cover the bottom. Put in the fish from Step 1, and shallow-fry it until crisp. When both sides are browned, take out and drain off the oil. Discard all but 2 tablespoons of the oil left in the frying pan.

3 Heat the oil again and stir fry the garlic and the finely chopped white parts of the scallions. When the oil is fragrant, add the tomatoes. Stir fry until the skins are curling up off the tomatoes, and add the pickled greens. When the moisture from the pickled greens has evaporated and they are coated in the oil, add the water and bring to a boil. Simmer over low heat for 2 to 3 minutes, then add the **Seasoning**. Add the fish, cover with a lid and steam-cook for 2 to 3 minutes.

4 Serve with dill and the green parts of the scallions on top.

CHEF'S TIPS

If you're using very salty pickled greens, soak them overnight while changing the water several times, and taste the sauce before adding all the nước mắm from the Seasoning, so that the sauce doesn't get too salty.

PUB FOOD & BAR SNACKS

Bia hơi is old-style Vietnamese draught beer.

Beer in Vietnam

A Love Affair with Beer

Beer accounts for 97% of the alcohol consumed in Vietnam. That's how much the people of Vietnam love beer. It's drunk at pubs and at weddings. At banquets there are cases of beer next to the tables, and the guests just help themselves.

Pub Crawls

The quintessential Vietnamese beer is bia hơi, a draught beer that's low in alcohol, (around 3%) and is often drunk over ice. Restaurants or drinking places that serve bia hơi are typically casual establishments where you can enjoy snacks like fried peanuts, boiled pig ears, rice-flour-coated fried shrimp (page 111) or French fries and bitter melon with flaked fish (page 115). Since bia hơi is cheap and low in alcohol, you always hear voices calling for "another round!" Another characteristic of drinking parties in Vietnam is that there are several rounds of toast-making. People often make a toast right in the middle of a conversation, which can be surprising, but it's a typical thing in Vietnam.

Vietnamese Craft Beer

Even though old-school bia hơi places are as popular as ever, what's really trendy in Vietnam now are craft beers. There are microbreweries all over the country, some earning prizes at international beer competitions. Besides pilsners, pale ales, IPAs and stouts, there's jasmine-flower-scented beer and a version called phở beer that's made with the spices used in phở soup like cinnamon and ginger. And since so many types of fruit are grown in Vietnam, fruit-flavored beers proliferate too. There are even chocolate-flavored beers. There are drinking places operated directly by breweries, as well as specialized beer halls that serve various craft beers. In the Vietnam of today, you can enjoy old-style bia hơi pubs as well as stylish craft beer halls.

Shinobu Ito A pub that serves beer (bia hơi) in Vietnam is called a quán bia hơi. The recipes in this chapter are the types of dishes served at these quán bia hơi beer restaurants. Bia hoi restaurants usually have a lot of items on their menus, from light snacks to full-on rather complicated dishes, even hot pots.

Yumiko Adachi At a quán bia hơi, you can get a range of dishes that go well with plain white rice, just like you can at a casual restaurant (see the previous section), as well as a range of small snacks that go well with drinks. Whenever I go to a bia hơi restaurant, I always choose them depending on their signature dishes. A lot of bia hơi restaurants offer seating in front of their stores, and having a light Vietnamese beer under a starry sky while nibbling on some appetizers is a memorable experience.

Masumi Suzuki I can't drink alcohol, but when I was studying in Vietnam, I used to go out for dinner in the evening with friends who liked to drink at bia hơi restaurants. All eat-in restaurants in Vietnam allow you to bring in your own food and drink, so I used to buy some fruit juice (sinh tố) from a nearby juice shop, or some tea from a tea shop, bring it to a bia hơi restaurant and enjoy the food there with my non-alcoholic beverage.

Garlic-Fried Bar Nuts Lạc rán

Masumi Suzuki

A standard drinking snack. On a hot day, a beer and these crispy garlic-flavored peanuts are a match made in heaven.

Makes about ½ lb (250 g)

1½ cups (200 g) peanuts
Salt, to taste
2 garlic cloves, peeled and crushed
Oil, for deep frying, at room temperature

1 Put the peanuts, crushed garlic clove and oil in a pan. Heat slowly over low for 15 to 20 minutes, to fry the peanuts. If it looks like the garlic is going to burn, take it out.
2 Raise the oil temperature to 340°F (170°C) at the end to crisp up the peanuts. Take the peanuts out, drain the oil thoroughly and sprinkle with salt.

Lemongrass Fried Shrimp Tôm chiên muối sả

Masumi Suzuki

These crispy shrimp are fried in oil that's been scented with lemongrass. The crispy fried lemongrass is mixed with the shrimp.

Serves 4 to 6

2 tablespoons minced lemongrass
8 tablespoons vegetable oil
20 whole medium shrimp (½ lb/220 g) with their
  heads on
Rice flour
Vegetable oil, for frying
½ teaspoon salt
Lime wedges

1 Put the lemongrass and vegetable oil in a small frying pan and heat. When the lemongrass has turned a very light brown, strain the oil through a fine mesh sieve. Reserve the fried lemongrass and oil separately.
2 Clean the shrimp. Dust them lightly with rice flour.
3 Put the scented oil from Step 1 and additional oil in a frying pan and heat to 320°F (160°C). Add the shrimp and deep fry until lightly browned.
4 Put the fried lemongrass from Step 1 in a small frying pan with the salt and heat. Add the shrimp and coat it with the lemongrass and salt. Serve with lime wedges.

Fried Cheese Sticks Phô mai que

Yumiko Adachi

Processed cheese is cut into sticks, breaded and deep fried. They're served with a hot chili sauce that will keep you coming back for more.

Serves 4

8 sticks processed cheese (⅓ lb/175 g)
4 tablespoons cake or all-purpose flour
4 tablespoon cornstarch
5 tablespoons water
1 cup (50 g) fine dry breadcrumbs
Vegetable oil, for deep frying
Hot chili sauce, to taste

1 Cut the cheese into 8 sticks as shown.
2 Combine the flour and cornstarch, and add the water to make the batter.
3 If the breadcrumbs are coarse, put them in a plastic bag and crush them to make them very fine.
4 Dip the cheese sticks in the batter, then coat with the breadcrumbs. Heat the oil to 340°F (170°C), and fry the cheese sticks until crispy. Serve with hot chili sauce.

Clams with Green Onion Oil Nghêu nướng mỡ hành

Yumiko Adachi

Nutty roasted peanuts and fragrant green onion oil are sprinkled over steamed clams.

Serves 4 to 6

24 medium littleneck clams (about 2½ lbs/1.1 kg)
4 tablespoons peanuts
4 tablespoons rice wine
Green Onion Oil (page 16), double the recipe

1 Wash the clams, removing any grit (page 113). Chop up the peanuts, and dry-roast them, stirring them around in a heated frying pan briefly. Take the peanuts out. Be sure not to burn them.
2 Add the clams and rice wine to the frying pan. Cover and steam-cook.
3 When the clams have opened up, transfer to a plate. Pour the green onion oil over them and sprinkle with the peanuts.

Chicken Poached with Citrus Leaves Gà luộc lá chanh   Yumiko Adachi

The chicken is coated with refreshingly fragrant citrus leaves, simply seasoned with salt and pepper, lightly poached and served with a lime sauce.

Serves 4 to 6

Salt and Pepper Lime Sauce (page 52), to serve
1 red chili pepper, sliced thinly diagonally

Chicken
1¼ lbs (600 g) boneless chicken thighs
5 to 6 scallions (bash the white parts with the side of a knife)
2-inch (5-cm) piece ginger, peeled and thinly sliced
2 teaspoons salt
3 cups (800 ml) water
18 kaffir lime leaves

Sauce
Nước Chấm (page 16), to taste
7 to 8 kaffir lime leaves, tough stems removed and finely shredded

1 Put all the **Chicken** ingredients into a pan and bring to a boil. Turn the heat down and skim off the surface. Cook for about 20 minutes. When the chicken is cooked through, turn the heat off and set aside to cool in the liquid.
2 Cut the chicken thigh into ½ inch (1-cm) slices. Arrange on a plate and top with the shredded lime leaves. Mix the **Sauce** ingredients together and serve on a separate small plate, with the Salt and Pepper Lime Sauce with added red chili pepper on another small plate. Dip the meat in either sauce to eat.

Clams Sautéed in Chili Oil Nghêu xào sa tế Yumiko Adachi

Vietnamese Sate Sauce is a chili oil infused with lemongrass. Dip some bread in the juice of these sautéed clams for a perfect, simple happy-hour snack.

Serves 4

1 garlic clove, minced
1 tablespoon vegetable oil
20 Manila clams (see Note)
1 tablespoon water
1½ tablespoons salted butter
Black pepper, to taste
1 tablespoon minced scallion
Baguette slices

Sauce
½ teaspoon nước mắm
½ teaspoon sugar
½ teaspoon Sate Sauce (page 134)

> **NOTE** Rinse the clams under running water to wash them and remove any lingering grit. Use littleneck clams if you can't find Manila clams.

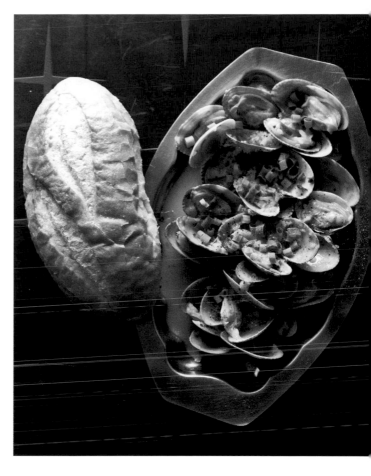

1 Heat the oil in a frying pan and stir fry the garlic. When the oil is fragrant, add the clams. Mix and add the water, and cover with a lid. When the clam shells open up, take the lid off and add the **Sauce**. Add the butter, and turn the heat off when it has melted.

2 Put the clams and sauce on a plate and sprinkle with black pepper and the scallions. Serve with the baguette slices, which are dipped in the sauce.

Chicken Gizzards with Ginger, Chili and Scallions

Mề gà xào gừng

Shinobu Ito

Crunchy chicken gizzards are stir fried with ginger and chili in this unusual bar snack.

Serves 4

½ lb (250 g) chicken gizzards
1 tablespoon rice wine
1 tablespoon rice vinegar
4 scallions
2 tablespoons vegetable oil
1 garlic clove, sliced thinly
1-inch (2.5-cm) piece ginger,
  shredded
½ small onion, cut into
  wedges and separated into
  layers
1 red chili pepper, sliced into
  rounds
A little black pepper

Seasoning
1 tablespoon Thai seasoning
  sauce
1 tablespoon oyster sauce
1 teaspoon sugar
½ teaspoon rice vinegar
Salt, to taste

1 Peel the membrances off the gizzards. Cut into ¼-inch (5-mm) slices and rinse in cold water. Bring a pan of water to a boil with 1 tablespoon each of rice vinegar and sake, and boil the chicken gizzards briefly to cook through. Drain, and rinse in cold water. Drain again, and pat dry with paper towels. Roughly chop the green parts of the scallions; bash the white parts with the side of a knife, and chop roughly.

2 Heat the vegetables oil and chopped scallions in a frying pan. Add the garlic and ginger, and stir fry until the oil is fragrant. Add the chicken gizzards and stir fry.

3 When the chicken gizzards are coated with oil, add the onions, red chili pepper and **Seasoning**. Stir fry while coating the gizzards. Add the scallions from Step 1, mix quickly and sprinkle with black pepper.

Beer-Steamed Squid Mực hấp bia

Yumiko Adachi

Squid is steamed in beer with a load of aromatics. So it's not surprising that this is another snack that goes perfectly with a beer.

Serves 4 to 6

1 lb (450 g) raw squid, cleaned, skinned and cut into ½-inch-wide (1-cm) rings
2 red chili peppers, sliced thinly diagonally
5 to 6 scallions, cut into 1-inch (2.5-cm) pieces

Salt and Pepper Lime Sauce (page 52), to serve

Steaming Broth
1⅓ cups (325 ml) beer
1 onion, thinly sliced
2-inch (5-cm) piece ginger, thinly sliced
2 teaspoons garlic oil (page 97)

1 Put the **Steaming Broth** in a pan and bring to a boil. Add the squid and red chili pepper. Cover, and steam-cook for 2 to 3 minutes.
2 When the alcohol has evaporated, turn off the heat and mix lightly. Add the scallions and mix, and transfer to serving plates.
3 Serve with the Salt and Pepper Lime Sauce, and dip the squid in it to eat.

Bitter Melon with Flaked Chicken Khổ qua chà bông

Shinobu Ito

Bitter melon slices are topped with Sweet Dry Flaked Chicken and served chilled. This is a new kind of drinking snack in Vietnam. Celery also works well.

Serves 4

1 bitter melon or 2 large stalks celery
Crushed ice
Sweet Dry Flaked Chicken (page 126), about ¼ of the recipe

Sauce
1⅓ tablespoons hot water
2 teaspoons sugar
2 teaspoons nước mắm
2 teaspoons lemon juice
½ teaspoon minced garlic
Red chili pepper, thinly sliced, to taste

1 Cut the bitter melon into 3 to 4 pieces lengthwise and remove the seeds and pith with a spoon. Slice about ¼ inch (5 mm) thick. If using celery, slice it into short, bite-sized pieces.
2 Line a bowl with crushed ice, and cover with cling film. Put the bitter melon on top of the cling film, and top with the flaked chicken.
3 Make the **Sauce**. Dissolve the sugar in the hot water, and mix with the other ingredients. Pour over the bitter melon and chicken to eat.

SALADS & VEGETABLES

In the South it's gỏi, in the North it's nộm. No matter which term you use, the fresh vegetables of Vietnam are front and center in these healthy treats.

Shinobu Ito Gỏi and nộm are dishes where vegetables are mixed with various seasonings; in English, they'd simply be called salads. At home they're usually made on weekends when people have time, or as an appetizer when there are guests for dinner. The key to the final flavor of gỏi and nộm is the prepping of the ingredients that go into it. Each one is flavored individually and then mixed together, so the more care you put into the preparation, the more delicious the final result will be. You can of course have gỏi or nộm at restaurants, but the ones made with care at someone's home tend to be so much more delicious.

Masumi Suzuki Whenever I go to a restaurant in Vietnam, I always order the gỏi or nộm. I'm especially fond of the sweet-sour salad that's topped with crispy fried shrimp crackers and shredded water spinach stems or lotus leaves. The thing that surprised me the most when I was learning Vietnamese cooking was the technique of massaging daikon radish and carrot with sugar to wilt them, as opposed to the salt used for the same purpose in Japanese cooking.

Yumiko Adachi In Vietnamese cuisine, it's considered ideal to have a balance of salt, sweet, sour, bitter, heat, fragrance, color and texture. Gỏi and nộm combine all of those elements on one plate. They always contain fresh coriander leaves/cilantro, and whenever I have one I think, this is what a salad should taste like.

Shrimp and Green Papaya Salad Gỏi đu đủ tôm

Masumi Suzuki

Crunchy green papaya and plump boiled shrimp are mixed with a sauce, and eaten on top of crispy shrimp crackers.

Serves 4

2 cups (200 g) shredded green papaya
8 fresh medium shrimp
20 shrimp crackers (see Note)
Vegetable oil, for deep frying
4 tablespoons fresh coriander leaves/cilantro, minced
Mint leaves, to taste
Fried onions, to taste
Nước Chấm, Version C (page 16), to taste

NOTE Try to get Vietnamese shrimp crackers, which are not spicy like Thai or Indonesian ones. Chinese shrimp crackers work well also. Shrimp crackers won't puff up if the oil temperature is too low, but they will burn if the oil is too hot. Try frying one as a test; if it puffs up immediately and floats to the surface without burning, the temperature is just right.

1 Finely shred the green papaya, using a mandoline or vegetable slicer. Put the shredded papaya in a bowl of cold water, then drain well. Peel and clean the shrimp. Boil briefly until cooked through, then cut in half lengthwise to halve the thickness. Deep fry the shrimp crackers in 340°F (170°C) oil until light and puffy.
2 Mix the green papaya and chopped coriander leaves/cilantro and put on a serving plate. Top with the shrimp. Add the mint and fried onions on top, and serve the nước mắm and shrimp crackers on the side. Add as much nước mắm as you like, mix up the salad and eat on top of the shrimp crackers.

CHEF'S TIPS

If you don't have a mandoline or vegetable slicer that can shred the green papaya very finely, shred it as finely as you can with a knife and sprinkle with about ¾ teaspoon of salt. When the papaya has wilted, rinse in cold water and squeeze out well.

Fragrant Beef and Spinach Salad   Gỏi rau muống thịt bò   Masumi Suzuki

Crisp spinach, watercress, lettuce and red onion strips are tossed with thin, quickly blanched beef slices in a spicy-sweet coriander dressing with crunchy peanuts sprinkled on top. What could be better?

Serves 2

¾ lb (350 g) very thinly sliced beef (see Note)
¾ lb (350 g) or 1 large bunch water spinach or spinach
¼ lb (120 g) or 2 small bunches watercress
½ red onion, thinly sliced
4 large redleaf lettuce leaves, torn into bite-sized pieces
Peanuts and fried onions, to taste

Coriander/Cilantro Pesto
2 bunches coriander/cilantro stalks
¼ cup (30 g) peanuts
1⅓ cups (300 ml) canola oil
2 cups (400 ml) Nước Chấm (page 16)

> **NOTE** Very thinly sliced beef cut for shabu shabu is available at Asian grocery stores. You may be able to get a butcher to slice it for you too. Otherwise, beef cut for cheesesteak can be substituted. To slice your own, freeze a block of beef for an hour, which makes it easier to cut very thin slices with a kitchen knife.

1 Make the **Coriander/Cilantro Pesto** by putting the coriander/cilantro stalks, peanuts and oil in a food processor, and processing into a smooth paste. Mix with the nước chấm.
2 Bring a pan of water to a boil. Have a bowl of ice water ready. Take single slices of the beef and briefly dunk them in the boiling water for a few seconds, then take them out and put them in ice water. Drain well. Repeat for all the beef slices. Put the water spinach/spinach, watercress, red onion and lettuce in cold water to crisp them up, and drain. Dry them all well.
3 Put the beef and crisped vegetables in a bowl. Add as much of the coriander/coriander pesto as you like and mix it all up with your hands. Serve topped with peanuts and fried onions.

CHEF'S TIPS

Water spinach and beef go very well together. You often see mixed water spinach and beef dishes at restaurants in Ho Chi Minh City. Very thinly shredded water spinach stems are sold at the markets in Vietnam, and they're often used as toppings for noodle soups, salads and mixed vegetable dishes. The Coriander/Cilantro Pesto here is my original recipe.

Vegetable, Pork and Shrimp Lettuce Rolls Cuốn diếp   Masumi Suzuki

A dish from Hue where boiled shrimp, pork and herbs are wrapped in leafy vegetables. Here I've used lettuce, but in central Vietnam mustard greens are sometimes used too.

Makes 6 rolls

6 large looseleaf lettuce leaves
¼ lb (120 g) very thinly sliced pork
6 medium shrimp
½ cucumber
1 bunch scallions, green parts cut into thirds
24 mint leaves
Nước Chấm (page 16), to serve

Spicy Mayonnaise
½ teaspoon doubanjiang (Chinese bean chili paste, available at Asian grocery stores)
4 tablespoons mayonnaise

1 Crush the central ribs of the lettuce leaves with your fingers to make them easier to roll up (**photo a**).
2 Bring a pan of water to a boil. Have a bowl of ice water ready. Take single slices of the pork and briefly dunk them in the boiling water for a few seconds, then take them out and put them in ice water. Drain well. Repeat for all the pork slices. Peel and clean the shrimp, and pierce them with a bamboo skewer from the head end to the tail end, to make sure they stay straight when boiled. Boil them in the same water you used for the pork, turn off the heat and let the shrimp cool in the water. Cut the cucumber about 5 inches (12 cm) long, de-seed and cut into thin sticks. Cut all but 12 of the scallions into 5-inch (12-cm) pieces. Quickly blanch the remaining 12 scallions until wilted.
3 Put 4 mint leaves, 2 cucumber sticks, and 3 to 4 pieces of cut scallions on a lettuce leaf. Top with a shrimp and a slice of pork (**b**).
4 Roll up the lettuce leaf while holding down the fillings (**c-d**).
5 Tie up the roll with 2 wilted scallions. Make two double knots to secure the rolls (**e**). Cut off any excess with kitchen scissors. Repeat for the rest of the ingredients to make 6 rolls. Arrange on a plate with the nước chấm and **Spicy Mayonnaise** on the side.

CHEF'S TIPS

This is special-occasion food from Hue in central Vietnam. It's usually eaten with a bean paste sauce, but it also goes well with rich mayonnaise and refreshing nước mắm too.

Pomelo Salad with Dried Squid Gỏi bưởi

Yumiko Adachi

Combine the refreshing, tart juiciness of citrus fruit with the umami of dried squid and the crunch of fried onion and peanuts. Dressed with sweet-spicy nước mắm and served with crunch shrimp crackers, this salad is a delight!

Serves 4

1 pomelo (about 10 oz/300 g) or 2 grapefruits
2 small (⅓ oz/10 g) dried squid (available at Asian grocery stores)
1 heaping tablespoon chopped peanuts
Fried onions, to taste
Coriander leaves/cilantro, to taste
Shrimp crackers or rice paper with sesame seeds, to serve (see Note on page 118)

Dressing
1 tablespoon sugar
2 tablespoons hot water
1 tablespoon nước mắm
½ teaspoon minced garlic
Red chili pepper, minced, to taste

1 Make the **Dressing**. Dissolve the sugar in the hot water, and mix with the other ingredients.

2 Peel the pomelo and remove the membranes. Pull apart the fruit into easy-to-eat pieces with your fingers.

3 Shred the dried squid, and cut into small pieces with kitchen scissors.

4 Put the fruit, squid and 2 to 3 tablespoons of the dressing in a bowl and mix together. Put on a serving plate and top with the peanuts, fried onion and coriander leaves/cilantro. Serve with the shrimp crackers or rice paper with sesame seed. Put the salad on the crackers or rice paper to eat.

CHEF'S TIPS

If you can't find pomelos, you can easily use grapefruit instead.

Flaked Chicken with Water Spinach Nộm rau cần ruốc Shinobu Ito

This mixed-vegetable dish is from the North. In Vietnam the dressing is served separately on small plates, for dipping the vegetables. It's easy to put too much sauce on unless you're used to eating this, so I've modified the recipe to add half the sauce to the spinach. The umami-rich chicken sauce is the star here, pairing perfectly with the spinach, sesame seeds and peanuts.

Serves 4

1 lb (450 g) water spinach or
  regular spinach
2 pinches salt
Sweet Dry Flaked Chicken,
  use ¼ of the recipe below
2 tablespoons white sesame
  seeds
2 tablespoons chopped
  peanuts

Dressing
1 tablespoon hot water
1 tablespoon sugar
1 tablespoon nước mắm
½ tablespoon rice vinegar
½ garlic clove, minced
Minced red chili pepper, to
  taste

1 Cut the water spinach/spinach into 1.5-inch (4-cm) pieces and put into a bowl. Sprinkle with the salt and mix. Leave for 4 to 5 minutes. Rinse off the salt and drain well. Squeeze out the excess water.
2 Make the **Dressing**. Dissolve the sugar in the hot water, and combine with the other ingredients.
3 Put the spinach in a bowl and add ½ the dressing. Mix well.
4 Portion onto plates and top with the flaked chicken. Sprinkle with the sesame seeds and peanuts. Mix the remaining dressing with 1 tablespoon water, and serve on the side for diners to add as they like. Mix the water spinach/spinach well before eating.

CHEF'S TIPS

Flaked meat is added to rice porridge, sticky rice and regular plain rice; it's also used as a bánh mì filling sprinkled with seasoning sauce and for dishes like the Bitter Melon with Chicken (page 115). It takes time to make the flaked chicken, but you can store it in the refrigerator and use it for the tasty dishes I've mentioned here.

Sweet Dry Flaked Chicken Ruốc gà (Chà bông gà) Shinobu Ito

This is a flavorful topping for salads and more. See the Chef's Tips above.

1 Slice the chicken breasts in half (**photo a**), and cut each piece into thirds.
2 Put the cut-up chicken and the **Seasoning** in a plastic bag, and massage the chicken over the bag to work in the flavors. Remove as much air as possible from the bag and close it (**b**). Leave it to marinate in the refrigerator for 3 to 4 hours.

3 Put the chicken pieces in a single layer in a large pan with the marinade. Add enough water to cover the chicken. Bring to a boil, cover with a lid and steam-cook the chicken over low heat for 10 to 15 minutes. Take the lid off and simmer for another 5 minutes over low heat. Leave the chicken to cool in the pan (**c**).

Makes about 3½ to 4 cups

1 lb (450 g) boneless, skinless
  chicken breasts

Seasoning
2 shallots, minced
4 tablespoons nước mắm
5 tablespoons sugar

a 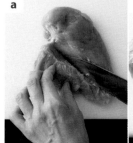 b  c

4 Take the chicken out and pat dry with paper towels. Shred the chicken finely with your hands (**d**). Rub the shredded chicken in a sieve to make it fluffy (**e**). The chicken on the left in **photo f** shows the chicken before it's rubbed in a sieve, and the chicken on the right has been rubbed.

5 Put the flaked chicken in a dry (no oil added) nonstick frying pan, and mix over low heat with a spatula until it's very dry (**g**). Transfer to a plate or baking tray, spread it out thinly and cool. Transfer to a storage container or bag, and refrigerate.

Stir-Fried Pork and Bamboo Shoots Gỏi măng

Masumi Suzuki

The refreshing fragrance of the lime leaves, the crunchiness of the bamboo shoots, the umami of the pork and the nuttiness of the rice paper with sesame seeds all somehow fuse seamlessly in this scrumptous creation.

Serves 4

½ lb (225 g) pork shoulder, sliced into thin strips
2 red chili peppers
Rice paper crackers with black sesame seeds, deep fried in 340°F (170°C) oil, to serve

Bamboo Shoots
1 teaspoon nước mắm
1 teaspoon sugar
Black pepper, to taste
6 oz (180 g) boiled bamboo shoots (canned or fresh precooked and vacuum packed), sliced into thin strips

Flavored Oil
2 tablespoons canola oil
1 teaspoon minced garlic
4 tablespoons minced red onion

Seasonings
2 teaspoons Thai seasoning sauce
2 teaspoons nước mắm
1 teaspoon sugar
4 tablespoons white sesame seeds
10 kaffir lime leaves, stalks removed and finely shredded

1 Mix the pork with the **Bamboo Shoots** ingredients to flavor it. Bring a pan of water to a boil, add the mixture and boil briefly; drain.
2 Put the **Flavored Oil** ingredients in a frying pan and stir fry. When the oil is fragrant, add the pork from Step 1 and stir fry. Add the **Seasonings** in the order listed.
3 Transfer to a serving plate and top with the red chili pepper. Serve the rice paper crackers on the side. Eat the salad on top of the rice paper.

VIETNAMESE HOT POTS

It doesn't matter whether the weather is hot and sticky or damp and cool, hot pots are always on the menu in Vietnam.

The Keys to Making Delicious Vietnamese Hot Pots

1. Cook the vegetables very briefly
Quickly blanch the vegetables in the broth.

2. Don't put the bún into the pot
When you're using bún rice noodles as one of the ingredients for your hot pot, don't put them in the pot. Everyone just puts some bún into their own bowl and spoons some soup on top. The noodles "cook" in the bowl.

3. Dip the ingredients in the sauce
Although the soup itself is flavored, sauce is always served on the side; the ingredients in the soup are dipped in it for extra flavor.

Masumi Suzuki Even in hot southern Vietnam, hot pots are enjoyed year-round. My favorite hot pots are the Lẩu Gà Rượu Nếp on page 136, a hot pot from the North made with a rice flour sake, and the mushroom hot pot on page 132, which is cooked in a Thai-style tom yum kung soup.

Yumiko Adachi Every region has its own hot pots; in the North they have freshwater crab hot pots, and in the South hot pots are eaten with mắm, fermented fish sauce. Many restaurants will let you choose the type of noodle you want. My favorites for adding to hot pots are bánh đa đỏ, a rice noodle that has sugarcane juice in it, and mì, Chinese noodles, or mì gói, the instant version.

Shinobu Ito Hot pots can be ordered at beer halls and of course at the restaurants that specialize in them. It's typically something one goes out for rather than making at home. It's also served to guests, and the last course at a wedding banquet is often a hot pot. There are so many in Vietnamese cooking you could make a whole cookbook of just hot pots.

NOTE 1 If you want to make your own chicken stock, this is a traditional way used in many Asian countries to make a clear, light stock. Put 2 chicken carcasses left over after taking off the meat in a pot with cold water to cover. Bring to a boil, drain and rinse the bones. Put the parboiled carcasses in fresh water to cover with 1 piece of sliced ginger. Bring to a boil, lower the heat and simmer gently while skimming off the surface for about 40 minutes. If the water reduces too much, add more. Strain through a fine mesh sieve.

Mixed Mushroom Hot Pot Lẩu nấm

Masumi Suzuki

A restaurant called Ashima in Hanoi came up with this hot pot based on the mushroom dishes of Yunnan province in China, and it quickly became popular throughout Vietnam. The soup of this hot pot packs a punch due to the umami of the mushrooms. Ground sesame seeds and peanuts are used as a condiment. In restaurants, the diners choose the mushrooms they want as well as the other ingredients and type of noodles.

Serves 4

4 large shrimp, preferably with heads on
¼ lb (120 g) very thinly sliced pork belly
2 oz (50 g) dried phở noodles
½ lb (225 g) water spinach or spinach, about ½ a large bunch
½ bunch (1 oz/30 g) watercress
½ head iceberg lettuce
Mushrooms, a variety (see Note 2)
7⅔ cups (1.8 l) chicken stock (see Note 1)
4 teaspoons salt
1 tablespoon sugar

Condiments

(per serving; multiply by 4 or however many people are being served)
1 teaspoon ground white sesame seeds
1 teaspoon crushed peanuts
⅔ teaspoon minced ginger
¼ teaspoon minced garlic
1 tablespoon minced coriander leaves/cilantro
A little red chili or cayenne pepper powder
½ teaspoon salt
2 pinches of sugar

> **NOTE 2** Here I've used 9 different types of mushrooms. Choose whatever fresh mushrooms are available to you. The more varieties you have, the better the hot pot will be.

1 Clean the shrimp, leaving the shells and heads on. Skewer them from the head to the tail, so that the shrimp stay straight when cooked. Soak the phở (see page 45). Arrange the shrimp, pork and phở on a plate (**photo a**).
2 Cut the water spinach/spinach and watercress into thirds. Arrange on a plate with the lettuce (**b**).
3 Remove the stems from the mushrooms, and slice into bite-sized pieces (**c**). Put the chicken stock and mushrooms in a pot with the salt and sugar and bring to a boil. Lower the heat and simmer gently for 10 minutes.
4 Mix the **Condiments** together and put on individual small plates (**d**). Start by savoring the mushroom soup as is. Next, put the condiments in a bowl and spoon in some soup (**e**) to make a dipping sauce. Quickly simmer the shrimp, pork and vegetables in the soup, and eat while dipping in the sauce you just made (**f**). At the end of the meal, put the phở in the soup, simmer until tender, and eat with the dipping sauce.

Chicken & Root Vegetable Hot Pot Gà nấu chao

Shinobu Ito

Bone-in chicken is flavored with root vegetables and fermented tofu and simmered in a hot pot. The leafy vegetables are cooked briefly to retain their integrity and texture.

Serves 4

1¾ lbs (800 g) bone-in chicken
4 medium taro roots (2 lbs/900g) or parsnips
¼ lb (120 g) lotus root or jicama
1 carrot (100 g) shredded
Water spinach/spinach, watercress, scallions, to taste
3 tablespoons vegetable oil
1 garlic clove, minced
4 cups (1 l) water
7 oz (200 g) dry bún noodles, soaked and cooked (page 45)
Additional fermented white tofu

Sate Sauce

6 tablespoons vegetable oil
2 tablespoons lemongrass, minced
2 tablespoons garlic, minced
4 to 6 red chili peppers, minced

Marinade

4 tablespoons fermented white tofu (see Note)
3 tablespoons sake
5 tablespoons sugar
1 garlic clove, minced
2 to 3 shallots, minced

1 To make the **Sate Sauce**, heat the oil, lemongrass and garlic in a frying pan. When the oil is fragrant, the lemongrass lightly browned, add the chili pepper and turn off the heat. Let cool.
2 To make the **Marinade**, put the fermented tofu in a bowl and mix it into a paste. Add the sake little by little to thin out the tofu. Add the rest of the ingredients. Marinate the chicken in this mixture for about 30 minutes.
3 Peel the taro roots and slice about ¾ inch (2 cm) thick. Peel the lotus root and slice about ½ inch (1 cm) thick. Put them in a bowl of water. Slice the carrot about ½ inch (1 cm) thick or cut decoratively into flower shapes.
4 Cut the water spinach/spinach and watercress into bite-sized pieces. Roughly chop up the scallions.
5 Put half the vegetable oil in a pan with the garlic and heat. When the oil is fragrant, add the drained taro root and stir fry until well coated in oil. Take it out of the pan.
6 Add the rest of the oil to the pan, and add the chicken from Step 1 with the marinade. Stir fry until the chicken changes color, then add the water and bring to a boil. Turn the heat to low and skim off the surface. Add the lotus root and carrot slices, plus the stir-fried taro root. Simmer until the root vegetables are tender.
7 Put the pot on a tabletop burner, and put the scallions and bún noodles on the side. Put the water spinach/spinach and watercress in the pot and cook briefly. Put some additional fermented tofu and sate on small individual plates. Eat the hot pot by dipping the ingredients in the sauce (a), or dissolving some sauce in the soup. Put the bún in a bowl or on a plate and top with the hot pot ingredients (b) with some soup (c).

CHEF'S TIPS

This hot pot is often made with duck meat in Vietnam. Use dark-meat chicken parts such as the thigh, drumsticks or drumettes (the thickest part of the wing). The leafy vegetables should be barely cooked. Be careful not to let the hot pot simmer too long on the tabletop burner, or the flavors will become too concentrated.

a

b

c

NOTE
Fermented tofu is sold in jars at Chinese or general Asian grocery stores. For this recipe the white kind is used, not the spicy red type.

Chicken and Rice Wine Hot Pot Lẩu gà rượu nếp

Masumi Suzuki

The chicken is fall-off-the-bone tender in this hot pot with a slightly sweet broth. Coriander leaves/cilantro and scallions are added and simmered briefly before eating.

Serves 4

2 lbs (900 g) bone-in chicken thighs, chopped into 2–3 pieces per thigh
Water, to parboil the chicken
1-inch (2.5-cm) piece ginger, peeled and sliced
10 cups (2.4 l) water
1⅔ cups (400 ml) Vietnamese rice vodka (such as Nếp Mới)
3⅓ cups (800 ml) amazake
1 heaping tablespoon salt
3 oz (70 g) bún noodles
Mustard greens, scallions, coriander leaves/cilantro, chopped, to taste
Shredded ginger, to taste

Lime Sauce
Salt and Pepper Lime Sauce (page 78)
4 to 5 kaffir lime leaves, stems removed and finely shredded

Chili-Sesame Sauce
Thai seasoning sauce, to taste
Sesame oil, to taste
Chili powder or cayenne pepper powder, to taste

1 Put the chicken pieces in a pan with enough water to cover. Bring to a boil. When the chicken changes color, take it out of the pan and rinse under running water.

2 In another pot, add the parboiled chicken, ginger and the water. Bring to a boil and skim the surface. Add the rice vodka and bring to a boil again. Simmer over low heat for about 30 minutes, to evaporate most of the alcohol. Add the amazake and bring back to a boil. Add the salt.

3 Soak and boil the bún (see page 45) and arrange on a plate with the mustard greens, scallions and coriander leaves/cilantro. Mix the two **Sauces** separately, and put on individual plates on the side as dipping sauces.

4 Transfer the Step 2 pot to a tabletop burner. Add the Step 3 vegetables and simmer briefly to eat. Dip the chicken in the sauce of your choice (**photo a**). Don't put the bún in the pot, but put it in your bowl as you eat, with the soup ladled over it (**b**).

CHEF'S TIPS

This hot pot is typically made with the lees or dregs left over after making rice vodka, but here I've used a Vietnamese rice vodka plus amazake to recreate that flavor. You can either quickly simmer the greens or just put them in your bowl and ladle hot soup over them.

NOTE Nếp Mới is a distilled liquor-like vodka made with yellow short-grain rice, plus fennel, cinnamon and other aromatic spices. It has a rich, deep flavor. If you can't find it, use kaoliang or maotai.

NOTE Amazake is a sweet fermented rice beverage. It is either non-alcoholic or mildly alcoholic. It's available at Asian or Japanese grocery stores. If you can, use a type that has no added sugar.

Mixed Seafood and Chicken Hot Pot Lẩu cháo

Yumiko Adachi

The base of this hot pot is a mixed-grain porridge with chicken, seafood and root vegetables added for a rich and satisfying flavor.

Serves 3 to 4

⅓ cup (90 g) uncooked rice
2 tablespoons brown rice
¼ cup (50 g) pearl barley
3 quarts (3 l) water
½ lb (240 g) boneless chicken thighs, cut into bite-sized pieces
½ lb (240 g) daikon radish, cut into quarters and sliced
1 large carrot (4 oz/120 g), sliced into rounds or cut into flower shapes
½ lb (240 g) kabocha or butternut squash, cut into cubes
1 teaspoon salt
2 teaspoon sugar
3 tablespoon nước mắm
4 pieces fried tofu (see Note)
5 or 6 scallions
12 Manila clams or small littleneck clams
8 medium-sized shrimp
2 to 3 types of mushrooms, about 1¼ lbs total (525 g)
Few stalks watercress or celery
Salt and Pepper Lime Sauce (page 78), to serve
Thai seasoning sauce, to serve
Red chili pepper, to serve

CHEF'S TIPS

In Vietnam, there are rice-porridge hot pots where the ingredients are added to the porridge and eaten with it. This recipe is a recreation from memory of a mixed-grain-porridge hot pot I had in Hanoi long ago. Some restaurants serve this with a white-rice-porridge base too.

NOTE The fried tofu used here is flat-fried tofu, also known as aburaage, tofu skins or tofu pouches. Small ones are called tofu puffs or soy puffs. Variations of this fried soy product are available at Asian grocery stores, and any of them will work.

1 Rinse the rice and drain in a fine mesh sieve. Put the white rice, brown rice and barley in a pot and dry-roast the grains while stirring for a few minutes. Add the water and cook for 15 to 20 minutes.

2 Take the rice, grains and barley out (if you leave them in, they will get too soft and disintegrate, making the soup too thick). Add the chicken, daikon radish and carrot to the pot and simmer for 15 minutes.

3 Add the squash and simmer for another 8 to 10 minutes. Add the salt, sugar and nước mắm.

4 Panfry the tofu, without adding any oil, until crispy, and rip it up into bite-sized pieces with your hands. (If using small tofu puffs, cut them in half.) Finely chop two of the scallions, and cut up the rest into 3-inch-long (8-cm) pieces.

5 Rinse the clams under running water and remove any grit (see page 113). Peel and clean the shrimp, leaving the tails on. Rinse the mushrooms quickly and shred into easy-to-eat pieces. Trim the ends off the watercress/celery and cut into short lengths.

6 Add half the rice, mixed grains and barley that were taken out in Step 2 back to the pot. Have the rest in reserve to add as the hot pot is eaten. Add the fried tofu, chopped scallions, fried onion and black pepper, and put the pot on a tabletop cooker. Put the Step 5 ingredients on a plate and serve alongside the hot pot. Serve the two sauces in separate individual plates.

7 Add the Step 5 ingredients a little at a time to the pot as everyone eats out of it. You can eat it with the porridge (**photo a**), or dip the ingredients in the sauces as you like (**b**).

RICE DISHES

These treats, made with short-grain sticky rice or long-grain rice, are eaten for breakfast or as snacks.

Masumi Suzuki There are so many delicious rice dishes in Vietnam: mixed-rice dishes like the Hue-style Cơm âm Phủ (page 142), rice with soup ladled on top like the Cơm Hến (page 147), sticky rice dishes and rice porridge. It's hard to choose. I'm especially fond of the dish called cơm lam, made by an ethnic minority that lives in the mountains. It's cooked in a hollow piece of bamboo. Eaten with sesame salt and peanuts, it's really addictive.

Shinobu Ito In Vietnam, sticky rice is made with short-grain Indica-type rice, which has a lighter texture. Rice porridge is often eaten for breakfast, as well as for a snack. Sticky rice is often available at speciality restaurants, as well as from street carts. There are light types mixed with peanuts as well as hearty ones with stewed pork belly or boiled chicken. A rice dish I'm really into these days is Cháo Mực Khô, porridge made with dried squid (page 146). There are a wide variety of rice porridges such as chicken porridge and seafood porridge, which you can eat from food stalls and street carts as well as at specialized restaurants.

Yumiko Adachi There's a restaurant I go to often for breakfast that offers noodle soups. I always order one portion of sticky rice with an herb-filled noodle soup on the side. I often eat sticky rice as a snack too. At one of my favorite chè (sweet soup and pudding) places, they have sticky rice with fried chicken, so I always have that before having chè. A single portion of sticky rice is always small, so it can be eaten with something else.

The Varieties of Vietnamese Rice

Masumi Suzuki

A Rainbow of Flavors

One of the world's leading export-
ers of rice, Vietnam has two major
rice-growing regions: the Mekong delta in the South and the Red River delta
in the North. The people of Vietnam
compare their country to a scale with
two baskets overflowing with rice.

Rice crosses the spectrum and
comes in a rainbow of flavors. There's
white medium-grain rice as well as
short-grain or mochi rice, plus black,
red and purple varieties too. The
fragrant rices called gạo tám cổ ngỗng
and gạo tám xoan grown in the northern province of Hà Nam are especially
regarded. Yet the most prized type of
rice is gạo tám cổ ngỗng, eaten at the lunar new year or other special occasions only. In the
past, it was only available in the cities. Gạo tám xoan has smaller grains than gạo tám cổ
Ngỗng, and was also mainly served to guests or given as gifts.

When you're eating fragrant rice, it's the rice that's the star, so don't serve strong-flavored
vegetables, seasonings, spices or pickles with it. The stir-fried beef and celery (Rau cần xào
thịt bò) on page 105, the preserved shrimp called tép and crab eggs stir fried with nước mắm
are ideal accompaniments.

Green Rice Signals the Start of Fall

In Hanoi, women from the village of Vòng arrive
selling cốm in baskets balanced on poles. Cốm is
made with short-grain or mochi rice harvested while
it's still green and immature. The grains are soaked
in water; the ones that float to the surface are too
immature and discarded. The remaining grains, at the
bottom of the water, are roasted and hulled in a large
pot. After the husks are removed, the bright green
cốm emerges. They say that in the past, in the wedding season of September, the new groom would send
a gift of cốm from Vòng to his bride's family. Cốm is
eaten as is, mixed with bananas, stir-fried with pork,
used in sweet chè or steamed and made into savory
sticky-rice dishes.

Hue-Style Mixed "Purgatory" Rice Cơm âm phủ

Masumi Suzuki

A mixed-rice dish made with pork marinated with lemongrass, shredded egg, vegetables and herbs. Everything is tossed together like a salad.

Serves 2

¼ lb (100 g) pork shoulder, cut into ⅓-inch (1-cm) strips
2 teaspoons sesame oil
2 beaten eggs
½ teaspoon each salt and sugar
½ cucumber
1½ cups (300 g) cold cooked plain rice
Green Onion Oil (page 16), two batches
2 large looseleaf lettuce leaves, shredded
Shrimp flakes (page 82), 8 shrimp worth
Daikon Radish and Carrot Marinated in Nước Chấm (page 17), to taste
10 cilantro/coriander stalks, chopped roughly
Nước Chấm, Version C (page 16), two batches

Seasoning
1 tablespoon minced lemongrass
1 teaspoon minced garlic
½ cup (20 g) minced red onion
2 teaspoons nước mắm
2 teaspoons Thai seasoning sauce
½ teaspoon black pepper

1 Marinate the pork in the **Seasoning** for 15 to 20 minutes. Heat the sesame oil in a frying pan, and stir fry the pork.
2 Make the egg crêpes. Add the salt and sugar to the beaten egg. Lightly oil a nonstick frying pan, and pour in a quarter the egg mixture, swirling it around. Cook over low heat until set, flip over and briefly cook the other side. Take out of the pan. Repeat with the rest of the egg. Shred the egg crêpes.
3 Peel the cucumber, remove the seeds with a spoon and cut into ¼-inch (5-mm) slices.
4 Put the rice in the middle of a plate, and pour the Green Onion Oil over it. Add the pork, egg crêpes and cucumber around it, along with the shredded lettuce, shrimp flakes, Daikon Radish and Carrot Marinated in Nước Chấm and chopped coriander leaves/cilantro. Serve the nước chấm on the side. Pour on some of the nước chấm (**photo a**) and mix well (**b-c**). Serve in individual bowls; the diners can add more nước chấm to taste.

CHEF'S TIPS

This dish originates from a restaurant in Hue called Quan Com Âm Phủ. That's actually a nickname, since âm phủ means "cemetery." The legend goes that the restaurant was near a cemetery or on a street associated with supernatural sightings. This is why cơm âm phủ is often described as "purgatory rice" in English. You can eat this dish at Hue-style restaurants in Ho Chi Minh City too.

Sticky Rice Fried Chicken

Xôi gà rô ti   Masumi Suzuki

Steamed short-grain rice with the sweet fragrance of coconut milk is paired with well-seasoned fried chicken.

Serves 4

1½ cups (300 g) uncooked short-grain rice
Water, for the rice
3 tablespoons coconut milk
3 tablespoons water
8 chicken drumettes
Oil, for deep frying
Fried onions, to taste
Daikon Radish and Carrot Marinated in Nước Chấm (page 17), to serve

Sauce

2½ tablespoons nước mắm
2 tablespoons lemon juice
2 tablespoons sweet chili sauce
3 tablespoons sugar
5 sprigs coriander leaves/cilantro, minced
½ stalk lemongrass, minced

1 Rinse the rice quickly, drain and put into a bowl. Add enough water to cover, and refrigerate overnight.
2 Heat some water in a wok with a bamboo steamer on top. Line the steamer with a damp kitchen towel. Drain the rice, put it on the kitchen towel and wrap the ends of the kitchen towel around it. Steam for about 30 minutes. Mix the coconut milk and water together. Every 10 minutes, sprinkle one-third of the coconut milk-water mixture on the rice.
3 Put the chicken drumettes in 285°F (140°C) oil, and gradually raise the temperature of the oil. Take about 10 minutes to slowly raise the temperature to 355°F (180°C). When the chicken is browned and crispy, take it out of the oil and drain well. Mix the **Sauce** ingredients together and add to the piping hot chicken.
4 Put the steamed rice on a plate, top with fried onions. Serve with Daikon Radish and Carrot Marinated in Nước Chấm on the side.

Flaked Chicken Sticky Rice

Xôi ruốc   Shinobu Ito

This is another standard way to eat sticky rice. The flaked chicken brings a subtle umami flavor to the table.

Northern-Style Chicken Sticky Rice (page 145)
Sweet Dry Flaked Chicken (page 126)
Northern Vietnamese Style Pickles (page 16), to serve
Thai seasoning sauce, to serve

Serve the sticky rice topped with flaked chicken and the marinated vegetables and seasoning sauce on the side.

Sticky Rice with Liver Pâté

Xôi patê   Shinobu Ito

Short-grain rice cooked in chicken broth is topped with liver pâté. The rice goes amazingly well with the pâté.

Northern-Style Chicken Sticky Rice (page 145)
Chicken Liver Pâté (page 72)
Northern Vietnamese-Style Pickles (page 16), to serve
Thai seasoning sauce, to serve

Top the rice with the pâté, and serve with the marinated vegetables and seasoning sauce on the side.

Northern-Style Chicken Sticky Rice Xôi gà miền Bắc Shinobu Ito

Short-grain rice is cooked in the liquid used to poach the chicken, then served topped with the cooked chicken. The refreshing fragrance of the lime leaves whets your appetite.

Serves 4

1½ lbs (700 g), bone-in chicken breasts (about 2, cut in half)
4 scallions, white parts only (bashed with a knife)
1½ teaspoon salt
1½ cups (300 g) short-grain Indica rice
4 to 5 kaffir lime leaves, stems removed and finely shredded
Northern Vietnamese-Style Pickles (page 16), to serve

Sauce

3 tablespoons Thai seasoning sauce
1½ tablespoons nước mắm
1½ tablespoons water
3 tablespoon light brown sugar

1 Put the chicken in a pan and bring to a boil. Lower the heat, skim off the surface, and simmer gently for 20 to 30 minutes. When the chicken is cooked through, turn off the heat, and leave to cool in the cooking liquid.
2 Rinse the rice and drain. Put the rice in a frying pan. Add 1⅔ cups (400 ml) of the chicken cooking liquid to the frying pan, and leave the rice to soak for about 30 minutes (**photo a**).
3 Bring the pan with the rice to a boil. Turn the heat down to low. Cook while stirring constantly with a wooden spatula (**b**), until the rice has absorbed all the liquid.
4 Heat some water in a wok with a bamboo steamer placed on top. Line the steamer with a moistened and tightly wrung-out kitchen towel. Put the rice from Step 3 on the kitchen towel, and wrap the ends around it (**c**). Steam for 10 to 15 minutes. When the rice is tender, turn the heat off and leave to continue steaming wrapped in the kitchen towel for about 10 minutes.
5 Put the **Sauce** ingredients in a small pan and heat until the sugar has dissolved. Turn off the heat.
6 Take the chicken off the bones and slice. Put the rice in the middle of a plate and top with the chicken. Pour on the **Sauce**, and top with the shredded lime leaves. Serve with Northern Vietnamese-Style Marinated Vegetables.

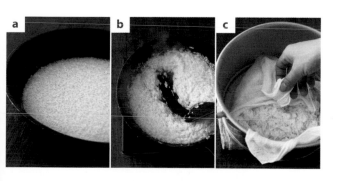

CHEF'S TIPS

I've used chicken breasts since they're easier to handle, but you can use thigh meat instead, if you prefer. By cooking the rice first in the chicken broth and then steaming it, it becomes full of flavor while still cooked through in a short amount of time. If you leave the chicken breasts in the cooking liquid until they're completely cooled, the result be amazingly tender and juicy.

Rice Porridge with Dried Squid · Cháo mực khô

Shinobu Ito

A rice porridge with a soup made from dried squid. Lots of shredded ginger is added to impart the light, refreshing flavor.

Serves 4

1 dried squid (about 4 oz/120 g)
5 cups (1.2 l) water
⅓ cup (75 g) uncooked short-grain rice
1-inch (2.5-cm) piece ginger, finely shredded
Nước mắm, to taste
Salt, to taste

Toppings
Chopped scallions, chopped coriander leaves/cilantro, fried onions, black pepper

CHEF'S TIPS

Dried squid is a common ingredient in soups in the South. If you grill it until it's charred and rinse off the charred parts, the flavor of the squid intensifies. When the rice is rinsed and exposed to air, it becomes brittle, and when it's dry roasted, the grains break up even more. Broken rice cooks a lot faster than whole grains.

1 Quickly grill the dried squid in a toaster oven or over a gas flame until slightly charred. Wash off the charred parts. Put into a pan with the 5 cups of water, and leave to soak overnight (**photo a**).
2 Heat the pan and bring to a boil. Lower the heat, and simmer gently for 30 minutes to make the soup. Take the squid out and cut into bite-sized pieces.
3 Rinse the rice and drain into a sieve. Leave for about 30 minutes.
4 Put the rice in a frying pan, and dry-roast (**b**). When the rice grains are dry, add the soup. Cook over low heat while stirring frequently for about 20 minutes.
5 Add the ginger and bring to a boil. Add the nước mắm and salt and flavor the soup lightly. Ladle into bowls and add the **Toppings**. Add more nước mắm or salt, to taste.

Clam Soup with Rice Cơm hến

Masumi Suzuki

Clam soup is simply poured over cooked rice, with lots of sesame seeds to add their slight nutty flavor.

Serves 4

1¼ lbs (600 g) small clams, rinsed of grit (page 113)
5 cups (1.2 m) water
2 tablespoons nước mắm
⅔ cup (165 g) cooked white rice
Red chili pepper, minced, to taste

Vegetables
10 stalks coriander leaves/cilantro, chopped
2 galangal shoots, chopped
4 looseleaf lettuce leaves, shredded
8 stalks rau răm (Vietnamese coriander or cilantro), roughly chopped
Mint, roughly chopped, about 24 leaves

Toppings
4 tablespoons peanuts
8 tablespoons toasted white sesame seeds
Pork rinds (page 83), to taste

CHEF'S TIPS

This is a dish from Hue in central Vietnam. It's made with freshwater clams from the Sông Hương, the Perfume River, which flows through Hue. It's usually made by pouring hot clam soup over cold rice, so the result is lukewarm. A strongly flavored fermented paste made with tiny shrimp called mắm ruốc is added to the soup.

1 Make the clam soup. Put the clams and water in a pan and heat. When the clams have opened, strain the liquid through a fine mesh sieve. Take the insides out of the clams. Return the strained liquid to the pan, skim the surface and season with nước mắm and salt.

2 Fill a bowl with rice and top with the **Vegetables** mixed together, the clams and the **Toppings**. Pour on the hot soup, and add some red chili pepper, to taste.

SNACKS, DESSERTS & DRINKS

Sweet or savory, these bites satisy a craving or stave off hunger pangs between meals.

Shinobu Ito Vietnamese people like to nibble on a range of sweet and savory snacks in between meals. The quintessential sweet snack is chè, a kind of sweet soup or pudding made with sweet potatoes, beans, grains and fruit. It used to be eaten warm, but these days there are iced ones as well. There's a bewildering array of savory snacks.

Yumiko Adachi When I used to live in Vietnam, a seller of tofu, carried in two containers on each side of a pole, would pass by my house every evening. I'd go out with a glass in my hand, and he'd put some tofu and ginger syrup in it. Snack foods are sold from hand-pulled carts as well as from bicycles. The amazing thing is that whether it's sweet or savory, you rarely get something that's not delicious from these street vendors.

Masumi Suzuki Snacks are sold all around town, all day long in Vietnam. Sellers of sweet snacks increase in the late afternoon, and there are always lots of sellers around the markets. I especially like eating chè at specialized eateries as well as from street vendors. A lot of eateries in Vietnam specialize in one thing, so it's fun to plan out your eating course for the meal, such as going to a chè place for dessert after checking out a new hot-pot place for your main meal.

Sticky Rice Patties with Seasoned Pork

Xôi chiên   Yumiko Adachi

Rice patties made with sticky rice are deep fried, then stuffed with stir-fried seasoned ground pork. This is a quintessential salty-sweet Vietnamese street snack.

Makes 4

⅓ cup (75 g) uncooked short-grain rice
1 tablespoon vegetable oil
1 teaspoon minced garlic
½ small onion, minced
¼ lb (120 g) ground pork
1 teaspoon cornstarch
1 teaspoon water
Oil, for deep frying
Hot chili sauce, to taste
Fried onion, to taste

Sauce
½ teaspoon sugar
½ teaspoon Thai seasoning sauce
A little salt
¼ teaspoon black pepper
3 tablespoons water

1 Rinse the rice, and cook on the regular setting in a rice cooker.
2 Heat the oil in a frying pan and stir fry the garlic and onion. When the oil's fragrant and the onion is starting to change color, add the pork and stir fry. When the pork is cooked through, add the **Sauce**, then mix well. Add the cornstarch, dissolved in the water, to thicken the sauce, and turn off the heat.
3 Divide the cooked rice into 4 equal portions, and form into patties. Use a round mold that is about 2½ inches (6 cm) in diameter to form the patties, if you have one.
4 Shallow-fry the rice patties in plenty of oil (**photo a**) until browned and crispy. Drain off the oil.
5 Make a slit into the side of each rice patty (**b**). Stuff with the Step 2 mix (**c**), and sprinkle with hot chili sauce and fried onion (**d**).

Banana Cinnamon Bread Pudding · Bánh chuối nướng · Yumiko Adachi

Baguettes are soaked in coconut milk mixed with egg until soft, then a delicous banana purée is added, and they're baked. Yum!

Makes 1 medium-sized cake

½ baguette (4 oz/125 g)
2 eggs
1¼ cups (300 ml) coconut milk
1 lb (400 g) bananas, plus 2 whole bananas
⅓ cup (100 g) condensed milk or cream
2 tablespoons salted butter
3 tablespoons sugar
½ teaspoon cinnamon powder
2 tablespoons cake or all-purpose flour

Coconut Sauce (makes about 1 cup/240 ml)
⅔ cup (160 ml) coconut milk
⅓ cup (80 ml) water
1⅔ tablespoons sugar
2 pinches salt
1 teaspoon cornstarch
1 teaspoon water

1 Rip up the bread into small pieces (**photo a**). Combine the coconut milk and eggs, and soak the bread in the liquid.
2 In another bowl, mash up the pound of bananas (**b**). Add the milk, butter and sugar, in that order, mixing between each. Add this mixture to the soaked bread in Step 1. If it's not sweet enough, add some sugar. Add the cinnamon and flour and mix.
3 Line a 9 x 9 x 2-inch (23 x 23 x 5-cm) square baking pan with kitchen parchment paper, and pour in the batter. Slice the remaining

2 bananas, and put on top. Bake in a preheated 400°F (200°C) oven until browned, about an hour. Cool in the baking pan (**c**).
4 Make the **Coconut Sauce**: Put all the ingredients except for the cornstarch and teaspoon of water in a pan and heat. When the sugar has melted and the liquid is bubbling, dissolve the cornstarch in the teaspoon of water and add to the pan to thicken the sauce and leave to cool. Cut the cake into easy-to-eat pieces, put on a plate and pour the **Coconut Sauce** over it.

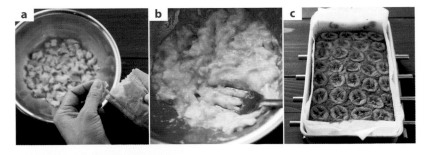

Steamed Banana Coconut Cake Bánh chuối hấp

Masumi Suzuki

Bananas are mixed with tapioca flour then steamed and served with a coconut sauce. The bouncy texture and rich flavor will make this one of your go-to desserts.

Serves 2 to 4

2 medium (250 g) very ripe bananas (the skin should have black spots)
4 tablespoons raw cane or light brown sugar
4 tablespoons tapioca flour or cornstarch
3 tablespoons plus 1 teaspoon (50 ml) hot water
White sesame seeds, to taste

Coconut Sauce (makes about 1⅓ cups or 330 ml)
1 cup (200 ml) coconut milk
½ cup (100 ml) water
1¾ tablespoons sugar
1 pinch salt
½ tablespoon cornstarch

1 To make the **Coconut Sauce**, heat the coconut milk and water in a pan. Add the sugar and salt and dissolve. Dissolve the cornstarch in a ½ tablespoon of water, add to the pan and thicken the sauce.
2 Cut the bananas into ½-inch (1-cm) slices. Sprinkle with the sugar and salt, and mix with a spoon. Leave for 15 minutes to absorb the flavors.
3 When the bananas have begun to release water and look shiny (**photo a**), combine the tapioca flour and hot water, and mix with the bananas (**b**). (Using boiling hot water for the tapioca flour helps it melt better, and the cake will steam more quickly.)
4 Transfer the mixture into a heatproof container (**c**) and steam.
5 Cool the cake into easy-to-eat pieces, and serve with the **Coconut Sauce** and sesame seeds.

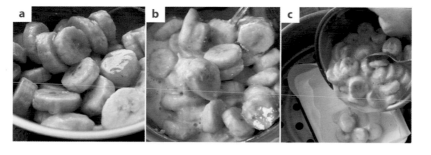

Crispy Honey-Soaked Bánh Mì

Bánh mì nướng mật ong Yumiko Adachi

A baguette soaked in honey is fried in butter until crispy. What could be better?

Serves 4

Two 8-inch-long (20-cm) crusty
  French style rolls or half
  baguettes
½ cup (160 g) honey
2 tablespoons vegetable oil
4 tablespoons salted butter

1 Flatten the baguette with a rolling pin (**photo a**).
2 Put the baguette in a shallow tray or baking dish, pour the honey over it and leave for 15 minutes (**b**).
3 Heat the oil in a frying pan, and fry the honey-soaked baguette on both sides. When it's browned, add the butter (**c**) and continue frying until the bread is slightly charred (**d**). Cut into bite-sized pieces and serve.

CHEF'S TIPS

In northern Vietnam, there are a lot of food stalls that sell charcoal-grilled chicken skewers. They also sell this sweet bánh mì. Crusty rolls are flattened, soaked in honey, put on skewers and grilled. The nutty fragrance, the crispy surface and the subtly sweet flavor are all very addictive.

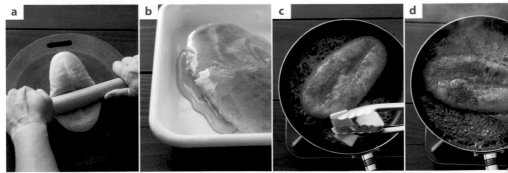

a

b

c

d

Stir-Fried Corn with Dried Shrimp Bắp xào

Yumiko Adachi

The sweetness of the corn combined with the umami of the shrimp and the spiciness of the chili sauce in this dish is irresistably delicious.

Serves 4

One 15-oz (400 g) can whole
　corn kernels or fresh corn cut
　from 3 steamed cobs
1½ tablespoons salted butter
1 teaspoon vegetable oil
1 teaspoon minced garlic
2 tablespoons tiny dried
　shrimp
1 tablespoon nước mắm
2 teaspoons sugar
1 pinch salt
4 tablespoons chopped
　scallion
Fried onions, to taste
Hot chili sauce, to taste

1 Drain the corn kernels well, and pat dry with paper towels.
2 Put half the butter, the whole amount of oil and the garlic in a frying pan and heat. When it's fragrant, add the corn and dried shrimp and stir fry.
3 Add the nước mắm, sugar, the rest of the butter, salt and scallions in that order. Put on serving plates, and add fried onions and hot chili sauce, to taste.

CHEF'S TIPS

This is a snack sold by roving street vendors, often from bicycles. They stir fry it for you to order, a great snack when you're hungry for just a little something.

Coconut and Peanut Dumplings in Sweet Ginger Syrup

Chè bột lọc

Shinobu Ito

Coconut and peanuts are wrapped in a chewy, springy dough and cooked in a ginger-flavored syrup.

Serves 4

½ cup (100 g) tapioca flour or cornstarch
Hot water
4 tablespoons peanuts (cut in half)
4 tablespoons coconut, shredded

Syrup

1-inch (2.5-cm) piece ginger, finely
  shredded
½ cup (100 g) sugar
1 pinch salt
1¼ cups (300 ml) water

1 Bring plenty of water to a boil in a large pan. Put the tapioca flour in a bowl, and add the boiling water little by little while mixing constantly with chopsticks or a fork (**photo a**). When the dough comes together, knead it well with your hands. Add a little more hot water until the dough is soft enough to wrap around the filling (**b**). About 5½ tablespoons of the hot water are used to make the dough; the rest is used for boiling the dumplings.

2 Divide the dough into 32 portions. Wrap each portion around a little peanut and coconut, and form into dumplings (**c-f**).

3 Bring the pan of water back to a boil, and cook the dumplings. Wait until they float to the surface, and cook for another minute or so. When they're puffy, remove from the pan and put into a bowl of cold water.

4 Bring the **Syrup** to a boil in another pan. When the sugar has dissolved, add the drained dumplings and simmer briefly. Serve in bowls with the **Syrup**.

CHEF'S TIPS

This is a classic dish from Hue. If you can, use fresh coconut to fill the dumplings, but here I use the dried shredded supermarket version; it's your choice.

Black Rice & Yogurt Shake Sữa chua nếp cẩm

Yumiko Adachi

A snack drink with sweet simmered black rice and yogurt, this refreshing treat is often served with ice.

Serves 4

½ cup (100 g) uncooked black rice
1 cup (200 ml) plus ½ cup (100 ml) water
Crushed ice
1 tablespoon toasted coconut
⅓ cup (50 ml) coconut milk
¼ cup (50 g) sugar

Yogurt Blend
½ cup (200 g) plain yogurt
2 tablespoons condensed milk
3⅓ tablespoons sugar

CHEF'S TIPS

In Hanoi, many street stalls sell a mixture of fresh fruit, coconut and condensed milk called hoa quả dầm. This is a variation of a yogurt-based mixture that's become popular in recent years. The texture of the black rice and the acidity of the yogurt go together surprisingly well.

a

1 Rinse the black rice briefly, and soak in 1 cup (200 ml) water for about 30 minutes. Add the remaining ½ cup (100 ml) of water, and put into a pan. Cover, and cook over low heat for about 25 minutes, stirring occasionally. Add more water if it's needed.

2 When the rice is tender and there's no moisture left in the pan, add the coconut milk and sugar and cook for another 10 minutes uncovered. Turn off the heat and leave to cool.

3 Put the cooked rice and the **Yogurt Blend** in glasses, and top with crushed ice. Sprinkle with roasted coconut. Mix it up well with a spoon (**photo a**).

Coconut Coffee Milkshake Cốt Dừa Cà Phê

Masumi Suzuki

This is a coconut milkshake, served with sweet-smelling yet bitter Vietnamese coffee poured on top.

1 serving

1 heaping tablespoon roasted
   ground Vietnamese coffee (see
   Note)
1 tablespoon plus ½ cup (100
   ml) boiling water

Milkshake
⅔ cup (100 g) coconut ice cream
⅓ cup (70 g) coconut milk
⅔ cup (100 g) crushed ice
1½ tablespoons condensed milk
   or cream

1 Brew the coffee, and cool.
2 Put the **Milkshake** ingredients
in a blender, and process until
smooth. Put in a cup, and pour
the cooled coffee over it.

CHEF'S TIPS

This is the signature drink from
a stylish cafe called Công Cà Phê,
opened by some enterprising
young people in 2007. A nod to
the Hanoi of the past, the shops
have now spread nationwide.
Coffee-drinking culture arose in
Vietnam as a legacy of the French
colonial period. There are cafés
across the country, where people
play xiangqi (a game like chess),
chat or just pass the time.

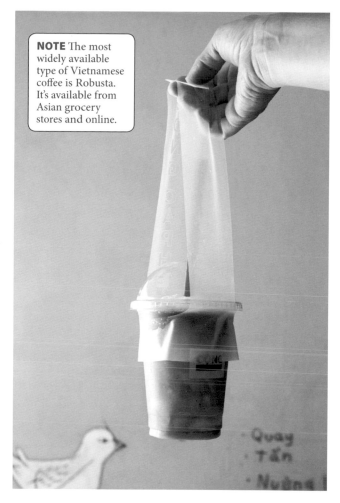

NOTE The most
widely available
type of Vietnamese
coffee is Robusta.
It's available from
Asian grocery
stores and online.

How to Make Unsweetened Coffee, Vietnamese-Style:
1 Start by putting the aluminum coffee filter on top of the coffee cup, and add the ground
coffee beans. Put the supplied inner lid on top (**photo a**). Add 1 tablespoon of boiling hot
water (**b**). Cover with the outer lid and leave to steep for 30 seconds (**c**). Take the lid off
and add the remaining ½ cup (100 ml) boiling water (**d**).

Published by Tuttle Publishing,
an imprint of Periplus Editions (HK) Ltd.

www.tuttlepublishing.com

English translation©2020 Periplus
Editions (HK) Ltd.

Original Japanese title: Betonamu Ryōri
Wa Nama Harumaki Dake Janai: Bēshik-
ku Kara Maniakku Made Oishī Reshipi 88
Published by Shibata Shoten
Copyright © 2018 Yumiko Adachi,
Shinobu Ito, Masumi Suzuki
English translation rights arranged with
Japan UNI Agency, Inc., Tokyo

ISBN 978-0-8048-5287-6

Original Japanese edition
Photography Haruko Amagata
Photography in Vietnam Haruko
  Amagata, Yumiko Adachi, Shinobu Ito,
  Masumi Suzuki,
Design Sato Yanai, Kumiko Sano
Cooperation Hisako Fukazawa,
  Sayaka Kakizawa
Editorial Miki Inoue

Printed in China   2307CM
26 25 24 23
10 9 8 7 6 5 4 3 2

"Books to Span the East and West"

Tuttle Publishing was founded in 1832 in
the small New England town of Rutland,
Vermont [USA]. Our core values remain as
strong today as they were then—to publish
best-in-class books which bring people
together one page at a time. In 1948, we
established a publishing outpost in Japan—
and Tuttle is now a leader in publishing
English-language books about the arts,
languages and cultures of Asia. The world
has become a much smaller place today and
Asia's economic and cultural influence has
grown. Yet the need for meaningful dialogue
and information about this diverse region
has never been greater. Over the past seven
decades, Tuttle has published thousands of
books on subjects ranging from martial arts
and paper crafts to language learning and
literature—and our talented authors, illustra-
tors, designers and photographers have won
many prestigious awards. We welcome you
to explore the wealth of information available
on Asia at **www.tuttlepublishing.com**.

Distributed by

North America, Latin America & Europe
Tuttle Publishing
364 Innovation Drive
North Clarendon, VT 05759-9436 U.S.A.
Tel: 1 (802) 773 8930
Fax: 1 (802) 773 6993
info@tuttlepublishing.com
www.tuttlepublishing.com

Asia Pacific
Berkeley Books Pte. Ltd.
3 Kallang Sector, #04-01
Singapore 349278
Tel: (65) 6741 2178
Fax: (65) 6741 2179
inquiries@periplus.com.sg
www.tuttlepublishing.com